Reflections in a Goldfish Tank

By Theodore Isaac Rubin, M.D.

FICTION
Jordi
Lisa and David
In the Life
Sweet Daddy
Cat
The 29th Summer
Coming Out
Platzo and the Mexican Pony Rider

NONFICTION
The Winner's Note Book
The Angry Book
The Thin Book by a Formerly Fat Psychiatrist
Forever Thin
Dr. Rubin Please Make Me Happy
Shrink
Emergency Room Diary
Compassion and Self Hate
Love Me, Love My Fool
Reflections in a Goldfish Tank

THEODORE ISAAC RUBIN, M.D.

REFLECTIONS IN
A GOLDFISH TANK

Coward, McCann & Geoghegan, Inc. New York

SBN: 698-10807-8

Library of Congress Cataloging in Publication Data

Rubin, Theodore Isaac.
  Reflections in a goldfish tank.

    1. Psychoanalysis—Miscellanea. 2. Psychology—
Miscellanea. I. Title.
RC506.R83   158   76-44534
ISBN 0-698-10807-8

Printed in the United States of America

To the young people—Trudy, Beverly, Jeff and Eugene
and their friends.

Reflections in a Goldfish Tank

*"I believe that man will not merely endure:
he will prevail."*

—WILLIAM FAULKNER—upon receiving the
Nobel Prize, Stockholm, December 10, 1950

Last night I was introduced to a man at a friend's house. When he heard that I was a psychoanalyst he asked me how one gets to really understand people. I told him that observation is all important, and of course this depends on one's ability to perceive. Judgment and moral equivocation: application of "good" and "bad" constricts, desensitizes and clouds perception. The power to observe is directly proportional to the ability to nullify the process of judging and moralizing. This involves a considerable struggle. We have all been taught over and over again to judge, to moralize, to qualify and to establish hierarchal positions. This absorbs time and energy. It also establishes prejudices based on old and fixed judgment values and vested interests. Associations to past experiences become more important than present encounters. Old pat-

13

terns are superimposed on new contacts and this, the antithesis of judgment-free observation, gives us little if any new information and virtually no growth. To suspend judgment is the thing because we are then unencumbered, unhampered and free to bring open total selves and energy to fresh encounters and to come away with understanding. This is not easy. Initially, considerable struggle is involved. The exercise is best kept simple.

"She has brown, large eyes. She talks quickly. She breathes deeply. She has thin, long fingers. She moves them rapidly. Her voice is high. She interrupts people often."

Observations of a more subtle nature will eventually reveal themselves.

"She touches people as she talks. Her hands are damp. She laughs and tears run down her cheeks as laughter seems to change quickly to weeping. She brushes her hair from her eyes with her left hand every minute or two, and raises her drink (straight bourbon) as often, emptying several glasses in the few hours I am in her presence."

I told him all this and he said he understood, but asked if the girl I described was anxious. I told him that his question was a conclusion based on judgment value. He said that perhaps it was, but wasn't it true anyway. I told him to trust his feelings enough to be open to them and to let them register without conclusion and evaluation and without developing pride and vanity as concerns their seeming truth. I added that vanity and pride in being able to perceive cripples the ability to perceive. He asked if I was able to do this. I told him that I was struggling to do this.

W e are trying to sell the beach house again and this reminds me of early feelings about death. These consisted of fear, rage and hopelessness. My earliest memory is the sensation and fear of eternal blackness. The frightening thing in this is not being dead at all, but really being alive in a black void forever. Now I know that the dread comes of the juxtaposition of life in death. Getting the feel of death, real death—"as dead as a stone," "as dead as a fossil"—gets rid of the fear of death because only the living fear death. But getting that feel involves a special, deep kind of surrender. It involves giving up the claim for eternal life and acceptance of that most human of human tenets, that life is finite after all. This is so hard to do when we are full of self-importance, and this lack of humility made for my rage and hopelessness. What good is it all, or what good is anything at all if that pervasive mortal flaw can never be eradicated despite any and all power, wealth, fame and glory achieved? But I enjoyed living anyway because I rationalized away the flaw. I remember telling myself that my children, like new leaves on a tree, would represent me even in a future which I would not personally share. Then I told myself that as long as any member of the species remained alive, a part of me would be alive, too. Aren't we all related? I told myself of memories people would have of me after I was gone—influences of me and ideas that I had and might even publish. But all these, including the monuments, only served as stopgaps and didn't work at all in anxious and depressing times. These were times of hurt pride, times when I was put in touch with the reality of human frailty and vulnerability. The worst as a child was when we moved because we couldn't afford the rent. These were times my father had to close his drugstore and more than that to take it apart and to sell off its stock and fixtures, because it was going badly. Watching them take apart the store was like dying. Selling the beach house is a different circumstance entirely. There's nothing desperate about it after all. We are selling it only because we hardly use it. But selling a house never fails to stir all this up, and buying a house always reminds me of my father opening a new store. These were times of birth and hope

16

and aliveness with much eating and drinking to cele-
brate—a kind of family fiesta and a salute to hope.

But the death business is somewhat better now. Realiz-
ing that dead is dead and not alive and trapped as in some
kind of eternal coal mine cave-in has helped. This has become increasingly possible as I've struggled to free myself of my egocentricity. The world will go on without
me, and its existence and that of anyone else no longer
rests on my shoulders. And yes I will die! Life is finite! I
will be forgotten—no leaves on trees and no representatives. My children will be their own representatives. I
suppose I am more accepting of the human condition
generally, especially of the all important fact of death.
This new found humility—feeling the fact that people
are only people and people die—helps. But each time we
sell a house—a little of it comes back and this is human
also.

It's about five years since my father died. I don't know the date or the day either. I think I've made a point of not remembering it. I can't see any point of remembering or marking a death date. We Jews do that—burn a candle to commemorate that day of the year. Some people don't talk or think about the dead. It's too painful, too anxiety-provoking, and so they blot out the good memories, too. My father's face flashes through my mind at least several times a day.

What I miss most are the wonderful fights we used to have. How I hated him! The yelling and bitterness, the intensity and aliveness and my mother on the side, wringing her hands, pale, terrified. We talk about it now and then and she still doesn't understand that in the middle of the rages—right there, smack in the dead center of even the worst tirades, we really loved each other. I tried to explain it but as intelligent as she is she again repeats that she doesn't understand. Our hatred was our only way of telling each other of our love. Love was too embarrassing for us to express or even for ourselves to feel. Our competition was too sharp. We were too inundated with frightening confusions about masculinity. We loved each other through fighting, and it's really that loving I miss now. Why does my mother resist understanding? Could it be that she doesn't want to give up a cherished memory of her role of martyred audience? My father and I were surely aware of what our fights "were doing to her." She told us often enough. What kind of a role did she play? When I look back I am a bit shocked to realize that we never fought other than in her presence. Indeed, without her about, we were great friends. We didn't speak of love for each other, but our conversations were always agreeable and warm and never led to any confrontations at all. But when she was there—a seemingly innocent presence—more often than not, just a few words or no words at all would flare into bitter and harsh diatribes. What kind of ancient or shall I say primitive ritual were we acting out?

In any case, we loved each other—my father and I—but even now it's not an opportunity to say "I love you" that I miss. It's not the agreeable conversations, either. I miss the fights and I'd like to have one now, without my mother's presence, this time, I think.

Theodore Isaac Rubin, M.D.

I passed a man on the street today who reminded me of Sam Land—huge face, big belly, enormous shoulders, deep chest, wide, thick hands. Sam Land, my father's best friend, a big man, a big life, a poor life. The big, the colorful part of his life was over by the time I was born. But I knew all about it from the stories he told and his conversations with my father.

Sam Land left Russia earlier than any of his friends and for several years wandered through Europe where he alternately became a member of groups of artists, actors, revolutionaries and zionists. Somewhere along the line he spent a few years in Turkey and was befriended by members of the Turkish royal family. I never found out what exactly his role was those several years, but the feeling conveyed was that of much intrigue, some violence, great love affairs and high adventure. Sam Land was a very powerful man, and he had a considerable temper, but he also had a wonderful sense of humor and was an extraordinary storyteller. He left Turkey to become part of the Jewish Legion which fought under the British in Palestine. He described Arab executions, slave sales, terrible battles, starving and suffering populations and all kinds of horrendous acts. He also told us of soldiers lined up in front of tent brothels in which two women took on as many as two hundred and fifty men in a single day. Sam was a considerable hero when he finally arrived in New York following his few years in the Legion. I know nothing of the dates, but only that all this happened before I was born. In New York Sam again took up his friendship with my father whom he knew since early childhood in the small Russian village where they were born. From what I heard, Sam spent most of his early days in New York with Jewish poets and writers of that time. Their social meetings mainly took place at the Café Royale in downtown Manhattan and quite often in whatever drugstore my father was currently trying to make a living. There was a considerable number of drugstores. I remember them talking about a friendship Sam developed with a waiter at the Royale. They played chess and provided much entertainment for my father and the rest of the group, telling about past adventures. During this time, Sam mostly eked out a living teaching Hebrew and giving occasional lectures on his Legion experiences. Sam's new friend eventually went back to Russia and the café crowd soon learned that the former waiter had become commander-in-chief of the Red Army. His name was Leon Trotsky. But when I knew Sam Land, all these were stories of the past. The Café Royale had been closed some years earlier.

I don't remember Sam ever having a place of his own—not even a room. His clothes were shabby, and he often needed a shave. From time to time he stayed with us, and if our apartment (we moved a great deal) was too small, he either slept on a cot in the kitchen or in the back of the store. I loved those days. We'd stay up all night drinking tea and some whiskey, too, and eating honey cake and herring and black bread. My father never discriminated on the basis of my youth or the need for me to go to school the next day. Indeed, there were days I just didn't go, and we'd have discussions with Sam and several other of my father's friends all day. My mother never objected, either. Of course to me Sam was a great hero, a hero rich in high adventure and lusty living on all scores. The fact of his poverty—and he was poorer than the rest of us in money, clothes, home, family, he had none of these—did not dilute my hero worship an iota. His size, his huge chest and arms were important, too, because throughout my teens I was tall and very thin. No matter how much I ate I couldn't gain a pound, and it was on this score that my feelings for Sam Land changed abruptly and radically one day.

I was fourteen and my voice suddenly became very deep. Sam Land had been wandering around the country and we hadn't seen him for several months. When he showed up one night, my mother made potato pancakes, and Sam told us of his latest adventures until early the next morning. But before I went to sleep that morning, Sam, almost as an aside, remarked about my voice. He said, "That voice goes with a big man. You're tall but you're too skinny to ever be big." That was it, just that. No one seemed to notice, myself included. I was tired and I went to sleep. But when I woke up late that afternoon my feelings about Sam Land had changed. I hated him. His uncaring freedom from involvement with the petty mundane business of making a living marked him as a lazy, exploitive sponge. High adventure became infantile, psychopathic ruthlessness. Huge appetites (food and women) became animal coarseness. Wonderful stories became gross distortions and lies. His gregarious vitality and ease with words became evidence of self-centered, narcissistic egocentricity. He was a ridiculous buffoon, a bag of wind. I write these words now. I didn't use them to myself then. But this was how I felt. The world which Sam Land had created had collapsed—had disappeared—had been wiped out and with it too had somehow gone whatever fairy tales and fantasies I had read up to then. His words about my voice had done it. I hardly knew it then, but they had done it. How? Why? Was my fantasy life so hooked to my pride (in being a big man—that idealized image of myself) that when my pride was shattered, it went too? Perhaps! But in that several hours of sleep, my feelings about Sam, about heroes and about high adventure died and what remained was anger at him and a feeling of unforgiveness. Unforgiveness of what—the remark? Yes, that and its effect on my own narcissism and also for bringing me into the very real mundane world—no more fantasy life!

Sam Land's visits somehow became more infrequent after that day. I made it a point not to be around when he did come. Eventually years passed that I had not seen him. Now and then I heard that Land had been sick and that he failed at some diverse attempts to make some money, including lecturing, a waffle and ice cream stand, selling books, etc. More years passed. I got big and heavy myself. Sam Land did not exist for me.

Then, one day, when I was in my late twenties, my father called and asked if I would go with him to visit Sam Land, who was dying in a hospital on Welfare Island. I went. He couldn't be Sam Land; he was just a thin, hollow-cheeked old man, lying in a bed which seemed much too big for him. The great voice was nowhere in evidence. The few words he spoke were terribly labored. Each breath seemed like his last. His few belongings—an old pair of pants, shirt and socks were in a small open locker next to the bed—not even a rented bed—a bed the city lent him. In that moment I forgave him! The Jewish Legion, the Arab women, the Turks, the mountains, the smuggling, the fights, the discussions, it all came back— born again in that few feet of hospital space. The wasted, poor old man died that afternoon and my hurt feelings and vindictiveness died with him. I think of Sam Land now and then and thank him for a childhood full of rich dreams.

REFLECTIONS IN A GOLDFISH TANK

I know that a mood, or shall I say a change in mood, springs from some rearrangement of internal emotional molecules. But it doesn't usually feel at all this way. It more often feels as if a particular mood is superimposed from outside. It feels as if we are going about minding our own business when out of the blue a mood drops down on us like a visitation over which we have no control and it hangs on. Once there, it is like a window which we cannot avoid looking through and feeling through should we want to see or to feel anything at all. And whatever we feel or see or experience is colored by that mood and so it goes with a mood of cheer and optimism or a mood of despair or the many in-between subtle ones. There are those of feeling old and heavy and others through which everything about ourselves seems young and light. There's the nostalgic kind through which each new experience brings up old memories and old and repeated associations. Yet, it isn't superimposed from the outside. The outside can only provide material—visions, ideas, sounds, smells, etc., with which to associate. But the associations come from the inside, and the kind of associations and whether to associate at all or to remain oblivious to outside stimuli—these too are all determined by the mood. Yes, sometimes something happens outside! A big change occurs, a big gratifying satisfaction takes place and the mood seemingly changes. I say "seemingly" because I find that it only seems to work this way. The real mood ducks out of sight for a while but continues to be there and reappears after stimulation by the outside event has petered out. But when the stuff inside of us finally shifts, when whatever struggle inside of us has finally taken place, the mood really changes and is then replaced by another mood, which eventually goes away when its time is over.

It was one of those dinner parties where people who never met before are seated together. It's an interesting arrangement which offers the potential to get to know new people. Ellie spoke to a former baseball player who quit the game entirely when he realized that he would never be the "best." He still longed for the game but could not bring himself to play. He told her that he used to enjoy watching the game, but he never did this anymore, either. It was too painful.

I listened and spoke to a young man and woman—he in

his mid-thirties, she in her late twenties. The subject of relationships came up. She spoke about painful relationships and wondered about avoiding them. He said that the main thing was to avoid opening up and telling people about one's self. He said that people finding out all about you makes you vulnerable. I asked him how this happens, and he said that he knew that it does even though he couldn't quite articulate the logic of it. I asked him how other people could hurt you with information about yourself if you refuse to hurt yourself with that information. He seemed puzzled, and I gave myself as an example. I told him that I had been extremely depressed some years ago and I told him and the young woman—she listened and said very little—most of the details of that depression and its effects then and subsequently. I pointed out that his knowledge of the personal difficulty I had gone through could in no way hurt me. Let him tell other people! Let him confront me with it. How could he hurt me if I refused to hurt myself with it? If I believed that nothing revealed about myself could cause me to blackmail myself, then I was free to reveal anything of myself to other people without the fear of potential hurt. We then went on to discuss the oft-quoted statement, "nothing human is alien to me," and the fact that all of the revelations of ourselves are human indeed. The young woman then said that *caring* could lead to being hurt, and we talked about the difference between telling about one's self and investing emotion in somebody else. A heavy and careless emotional investment can indeed lead to pain, but the degree of pain will here, too, depend

27

largely on one's loyalty to one's self. I then went on to explain how freeing it can be if we give ourselves the right to be rejected; how this is one of the great anti-hurt maneuvers. I described how most of us react to being rejected. We feel it as a blow to our pride (pride invested in always being accepted) and we then go on to restore our pride, which sets us up to be hurt all over again. We do this in one or both of two ways. We either lash out vindictively against the rejector, and if we score a vindictive triumph over the rejector we reestablish our pride position. Or we withdraw—telling ourselves we don't really care at all. The thing to do, I explained, is to struggle against the pride—to fight for the right to be rejected and to be rejected again and again and still again without hating ourselves for putting ourselves in a position to be rejected. Indeed, self-congratulation is in order for putting ourselves in that position, because once free of the pride, we are free to encounter life, to be open to tell of ourselves and to share information with others and to enjoy the fruits of what full encounters may bring. The young man asked why we would get hurt then if we invest heavily in someone else and it goes badly—"Isn't this the hurt of rejection?" I said that if it is the hurt of rejection, then it is hurt which comes of pride in always being accepted and in this regard of holding ourselves much too high. But if that pride has been vanquished and we still feel hurt, then we are suffering the hurt of loss, rather than hurt to self-esteem. This hurt which comes of feeling loss does not lead to vindictive maneuvers or to withdrawal but rather to renewed interest and involvement with other people so as to restore that which has been lost.

For a long time I've thought, or shall I say I thought I felt, the difference between intellectual understanding or an intellectual response, and a gut-feeling response.

For years now I've met men who found women with large breasts stimulating. I've also known many men, some of them my patients, who found women with small or virtually no breasts stimulating. Some of them said that large breasts were a "turn off." I understood this and thought I understood it on a deep down gut-level feeling, rather than just on an intellectual logic understanding level. I mean, wasn't this just a question of normal variations in taste? This could be due to cultural factors, background, era of upbringing, media impact, etc. What could be more normal than variation in aesthetic or sexual preference as regards different kinds of body types and attraction?

Yesterday I was walking on Third Avenue and a woman passed by. She was tall, slim, beautiful, and dressed in a tight satin blouse. The blouse could just about contain her very large, pointy breasts, which jiggled in every direction as she walked. In that moment I had the gut feeling deep down that no man who is "normal" could fail to find this woman and her bouncing breasts exciting. If she and her breasts are a "turn off," then surely the man in question had to have serious sexual problems.

After the impact of her more or less dissipated, I struggled to be rational with myself, using all the clinical experience and know-how I've acquired over the last twenty-five years. I told myself about taste variations, about variations in heterosexual proclivities, and so on. I recalled the many men I've known and treated who preferred flat-chested women and who never demonstrated particular evidence of sexual problems. Logically, it made sense and I understood. But then I thought of that woman again, and thought of her breasts under that satin blouse, and in my heart of hearts I still felt that anyone who found her a "turn off" must surely be sick.

All right—this does show me the difference between a gut feeling and a logical knowing. I've written about this elsewhere, but it is getting clearer to me. I also see how difficult it is to change a gut feeling even when that change is applied to someone else. After all, I am not asking myself to change my feeling about whom I find attractive. But why can't I feel other people as normal, even if they don't feel and react as I do? Are we so prejudiced then by our own experience? Is it the old story of not being able to see or let alone to feel—through the other fellow's eyeglasses? How difficult and yet how important it is to struggle with ourselves to let the other fellow feel his way without prejudice even if gut understanding continues to elude us. Otherwise communication is impossible unless experiences are identical, and since all of us are separate people our experiences can never be identical.

Theodore Isaac Rubin, M.D.

The water in my goldfish aquarium is cloudy today. Goldfish are members of the carp family and carp are supposed to be very hearty. But fancy goldfish are only hearty in their eating habits. They will eat anything, and, in fact, they never really stop eating. They are always sifting gravel on the bottom of the tank, looking for food. It's always a bad sign when they stop eating. But aside from their appetites, there's nothing I've ever found that's hearty about them. Wild carp have long bodies and short fins. The beautiful fancy goldfish, particularly the oranda lionhead, has been bred to have a short body and long fins. It therefore seems to me and to other people who keep these fish, that their organs are probably quite cramped, which makes them especially vulnerable to all kinds of fish difficulties. Anyway, cloudy water may be the result of a temporary atmospheric condition, or it can be the beginning of bacterial pollution. The latter can wipe out a tank's population in just a few hours.

All of this is interesting and since I once even thought of being an icthyologist I suppose there's a certain pride I've always had in my ability to care for goldfish and to contribute to their longevity. Again and again I've heard stories about their ability to live for years—even close to a hundred years. I've never had one who lived more than four years, but I keep trying. But however conscientious I've been to catch and treat ich, body and tail rot, swim bladder trouble, etc., in their earliest manifestations— these and what seems to me to be advanced age at an early age invariably win out.

REFLECTIONS IN A GOLDFISH TANK

For many years I have had a feeling about goldfish—and I'm talking about large, distinctive goldfish—which I've never had about tropical or saltwater fish. I see them as individuals and as being different in their behavior one from the other. I also realize I relate to each goldfish I have had for a while with real emotional investment. I can't imagine how they feel about me, but for me each is a real personality and I care about each of them almost as much as for my dog. Is this pure projection on my part? Do I imbue them, cold, dumb, blank creatures that they are, with my own particular needs to see them as I do? Perhaps, but interestingly other goldfish people feel the same way. Indeed, nearly everyone I've talked to says this about them. I have not picked up this kind of relating to fish in people who keep tropical or saltwater fish, and this includes those who have kept large, prize specimens for years. This seems to be so even though other fish—large oscars, discus, angels, and severim and so on—also learn to be hand fed and accept being touched. So what is it about goldfish? Is it their graceful movement, beautiful colors, large, alert but somehow vulnerable eyes, their peaceful proclivities (unlike most other fish they don't fight), their constant search for food? Perhaps some of us unconsciously identify with the last. Or is it that many of us have had small common goldfish when we were very young children? Is it because these small creatures may have been the first live entities in which we made our first responsible emotional investments? If this is so, how important the experience of this and other early attachments and relationships must be. Is it also because this was our first experience with responsibility for another creature and also the first confrontation with life and death of a living being? Because to the innocent and unsophisticated child, the little goldfish in the bowl (an environment in which survival for more than a few months is impossible) must surely feel like a person.

I remember feeling heartbroken about the death of each goldfish that I lost when I was three or four years old and being told that it was "only a fish," not a person, but "only a fish." I'm sure I shook my head in agreement. I even believed them. I wanted to believe them. But I felt otherwise. I felt deep sorrow, because a being for whom I cared was gone. But now, the feelings I do have for goldfish are always connected to large distinctive ones and while cloudy water still fills me with apprehension my feeling about them when they die is not nearly as strong as when I was a child. I'm sure we do get used to death and loss and our reactions do get blunted along the way. But why the big fish—why don't I react with whatever feelings I have about death of a fish, to small ones dying? I suspect that this is related to the vast embroidery we develop as adults. What I mean is that a simple goldfish is not enough to relate to, once childish innocence and imagination are gone. After worldly sophistication has pushed simple childhood reactions into near oblivion, at least a big and fancy and expensive fish is necessary for emotional involvement.

But much of the stuff of childhood survives. I still never feel committed to a new house to which we move nor is it complete until I set up a goldfish tank.

REFLECTIONS IN A GOLDFISH TANK

And when I look at that tank and take the time and try, I still remember a little of how I felt as a child. I remember the fantasy of being there among the fish, one of them in that cozy world, a world of fairies, elves and little clay houses. There was always a little Japanese clay house in the goldfish bowl. I lose the ability to feel now, what I felt then, when the water gets cloudy. Does cloudy water remind me of my current age and the real world we live in?

Today my patient, Nathan, told me that he can't think of any act between a man and a woman that is more intimate than sexual intercourse. I asked him how he felt about intimacy, and he had a great deal of difficulty coming up with any associations at all about that feeling. One of Nathan's great complaints about himself is his inability to get involved with anyone or anything on either a deep feeling or a sustained level. At best it's touch and run and mostly it's not even that. Despite himself, his holding back sometimes reaches the point of almost complete withdrawal. I asked him about sexual feelings and this too brought up very few associations, but he still said that sexual intercourse was the height of closeness. I just didn't and still don't have the impression that he was talking about how he felt (he has had sexual experiences), but rather of what he's heard—that intercourse is supposed to be "the most intimate experience of all."

I asked him about touching, and he became visibly anxious, and began to sweat, and I had the feeling that if we could pursue this line it would lead us to feelings he has about intimacy. But we couldn't! There was a block we just couldn't jump over or get around. "Touching" seemed to be a key symbol. It probably hooks up to all kinds of associations and feelings he does and doesn't want to experience, and I just couldn't get him past this conflictual spot. I tried, I encouraged, I explained, knowing very well that this last one—logic—never works and it didn't. He closed off and got off the topic completely and wouldn't come back. But I'm still on it and it won't go away.

Sexual intercourse can be most intimate, and it can also be a pretty cold business, too, and sometimes the most intimate time can be relatively unsatisfying on a sexual level, while at other times sexual feelings can be utterly requited without the presence of any real feeling of closeness at all.

I went into a burlesque show the other day. I saw one when I wrote an article on pornography and sex about two years ago. Things have changed radically since then. In the "old" days the audience was purely passive observers. This one was like no other show I'd ever seen. It was twelve-thirty in the afternoon. The place is in midtown New York and it was full. There were seats on three sides of the stage, and the general feel of the place was that of cleanliness and comfort. The tilting felt seats looked brand-new. The lighting system was good. Music was by tape and painfully loud. The front seats were very close to the stage and occupied by men from about seventy years of age. Some looked closer to eighty or even older. The rest of the audience consisted of men from about age twenty-five and up. Nearly everyone was well dressed. About a fourth of the people carried briefcases. There were no women in the audience. Admission was three dollars for this, the first show of the day. The show consisted of six attractive, well-proportioned girls, each of whom came out on the stage separately and performed her act for about fifteen minutes. It took three minutes for the girls to remove their clothes. Two of them took it all off and then spent the rest of the time bumping and grinding to the music. Occasionally they got on their backs, spread their legs and demonstrated considerable vaginal muscular control, opening and closing their vaginas with great rapidity. They then got on their bellies and all fours and did the same with their anal sphincters. The men applauded politely. No one made any attempt to touch these girls. The other four girls kept their stockings on, rolled up on their thighs nearly up to the pubis. This was a signal. Each girl, as soon as she stripped, stepped in front of each man in the front row for a minute or two at a time and leaned backward. The man stood up and tucked a dollar bill between her thigh and her stocking. He then reached around and holding her buttocks, one with each hand, brought her vagina to his mouth. He kissed and licked it and on occasion two of the girls separated the vaginal lips with her hands. She then leaned forward, which was a signal, and he stopped, reached up and sucked first one nipple and then the other. After the girl finished with the men in the front rows, a few men seated in the back came forward, tucked their dollars and did the same. Each girl left the front stage smiling and generally looking very pleased and the men applauded loudly. I saw some of them turn to each other approvingly and I heard a few of them say, "fine girl, fine girl," "just great, great."

Well what went on? Peculiarly, I didn't feel that there was much or any sex in what went on. The activities of the men and the four girls did not feel to me as sexual as those of the two girls who weren't touched at all. None of it was nearly as sexual as the old burlesque show in which the stripteaser spent her whole act removing her clothes and never showing either her nipples or her pubis. When the show was over, the old men, from the front seats, seemed enormously pleased. Certainly no sex act was completed. They seemed to be strangers before the show started, just staring ahead, silent, some reading newspapers. When it was over, they left the theater talking to each other and commenting about the girls—"how nice, how pretty." There was no evidence of coarseness or vulgarity and strangely—no sexual allusions at all! Well what were these men buying? I think it may have been intimacy! As fleeting as it was and even though they may not have consciously been aware of it—intimacy— on a safe, nonemotional investment, on a commercial basis, may have been what they got. The girls may have felt it, too, and the entire participation of each man before the others, an almost ritualistic act, may have made the men feel intimate with each other—even if only for the few minutes it took to leave the theater. But could the same intimacy, if that's what it was, have been achieved through language spoken or did it have to be through years of habit and other reasons, physical? And if so— could hands-holding or rubbing together have accomplished the same thing? Perhaps sex was needed or a play at sex in order to cover up feelings of intimacy. Perhaps public sex is less embarrassing than public intimacy. Thinking of hands, there are times when I feel more with the palms of my hands than with any other part of myself—mind or body—and touching anyone or anything at those times with my palms is the most intimate thing I can do, and at those times it isn't sex I feel at all. It is as if somehow in this way the center of myself feels touched. Does the other person feel it, too? I don't know. Truth is, I never asked. Perhaps this feeling of intimacy has been embarrassing for me, too. Is it important who the other person is or are we sometimes in a state of the kind of openness and free flow as to make intimacy with any other person possible? When it happens to me is it only happening to me—am I only using the other person or is chemistry between us an absolute requirement?

There is a chemistry involved, and yet I'm aware that I know little or nothing of what it is about. I suppose like the chemistry of sex, it's the result of a multiplicity of experiences and the interlocking emotional and symbolic associations of years. It seems unfair, somehow, that knowing and caring may not play much of a role and may even keep people apart in their deepest feelings. Maybe that's why the old men in the burlesque theater took an impersonal, sexual route with strangers, or did they attempt to use sex to break through a cemetery of dead feelings to live ones? What nourishment were they really seeking from those vaginas and breasts? Was it intimacy after all? I'm reminded of the prostitutes I interviewed when I worked as a prison psychiatrist in the Women's House of Detention. For some of them, sexual intercourse was the least intimate activity that existed. One girl blushed when she told me of dancing with a man who kissed her on the cheek and the closeness she then felt.

Maybe the old men deep down knew that it can't be done with words, with talking, but that physical touching has to be involved. Yet they used their mouths rather than hands. But I do know many people who reach out and touch as they talk and others who recoil and, like Nathan, always seem to be running away.

Theodore Isaac Rubin, M.D.

I stare at the goldfish this morning, and they, like me, haven't quite woke up. They drift about the tank, their long fins pushed this way and that by the currents of the filter and air stone. I don't remember dreaming last night, but I woke up feeling slightly anxious and out of sorts. Nothing I can pinpoint, just not as peaceful as I've felt other mornings. But watching the goldfish in their scene does it for me. I gradually come fully awake as they do, too, and concentrating absently—the water, the air bubbles and the fish floating by in the foreground, and my looking through that scene on to a hazy background beyond concentration gives me peace. I mean that my mind is on the tank scene; this is the concentrated part, and then there's the peripheral part that lazes along beyond that—a sort of peripheral vision—no sharp focus and no thoughts—no words. And I slowly come fully awake and the tension is gone. Perhaps this is why I've never put a small house in the tank as I've done when I was young. It would be a point of excess concentration. But I've also learned over the years that foreign bodies in the tank are hazardous. The fish scrape themselves against them and fungus quickly forms on even superficial abrasions.

Now that we are both fully awake I give them a few flakes of food. I would like to give them more. I don't like to leave them hungry. But however efficient they are in their super energetic quest for food, and even though I have a superb filter system, food has a way of lodging under the gravel and creating pollution. When I was in my

42

teens some of us invented all kinds of elaborate machine-driven filtration systems, but they always turned out to have grievous limitations. Some of them hardly worked at all. The current Eheim system is the best I could find, but even the best just doesn't provide the kind of clean water found in a natural pond or lake which hasn't been polluted.

When they had just about finished eating, I thought about them, especially Sam. Even as I write, there he is, still looking for food—hoping to find something left over? Hoping? Does Sam, my favorite fat friend, hope? Isn't he an instinct-driven creature who functions purely in accordance with instinct design? Yes, I see how he eats! But couldn't this, at least in part, resemble the food addiction compulsion so many of us humans have? In my feelings about Sam, highly prejudiced and subjective of course, I find it hard to see him as only a more or less complicated creature designed to obey built-in chemical commands. Even Sam must have choice. Perhaps not much, but at least a little choice in some issues.

But what of us, those of us who live in the other tank? More and more I feel that Freud was dead wrong in this regard. I've been writing a book about the human mind and I do some of it, put it down, feel and think a little more and pick it up again. It's a big job and hard work. My feelings about this issue of instincts will play a large role in that book about the mind. Freud felt that we are driven by instincts and suffer great difficulty and neurotic development as a result of repressing and denying instinctual needs. I just can't agree! I think we've

43

gone beyond instincts, and I feel that its lack of these chemical sign posts and our new found evolutionary freedom which makes us creatures capable of choice. This produces conflict, anxiety, and the development of neurotic patterns used as an attempt to cope with anxiety and conflict. Yes, unlike instinct-directed simpler creatures, we have to tell ourselves what to do and this is no small matter.

Sam has just found a small accumulation of food behind the right rear-corner filter-return tube. He's managed to suck it out, and I've noticed for months now that none of the other fish has ever "thought?" to do this. Is his instinctual drive for food stronger than that of the others? I doubt it because even now, they are all engaged in their endless sifting gravel search for food. They pick up a little gravel and then spit it out and keep whatever food may be left. They know the difference between what is and isn't edible.

Reflections in a Goldfish Tank

Why do these fish get sick? Seems to me that their resistance to any kind of onslaught is very poor. What kind of immunological systems do they have? Does it include antibodies of some sort?

I have a friend who is a Christian Scientist. He never talks about illness. He's convinced that talking about it spreads it around. I suppose he's really talking about suggestibility. But I haven't seen serious diseases either caused or cured by suggestion. Periodically, though, I've heard of people developing illnesses they worried about for years. Of course the illness may have run in the family, and this may have been the rational basis for both the worry in the first place and the disease developing later on. But I've also heard of various terminal, inoperable, metastic intra-abdominal cancers that suddenly underwent spontaneous cures. These have been validated by serious workers in the field. I remember one such case in the old Beth El Hospital in Brooklyn. A man had been operated on for stomach cancer. The spread had been too extensive, and they closed his abdomen having made no attempt to remove the massive tumor. He was given a few months to live but returned to the hospital years later for an acute appendicitis. When they did the appendectomy, there was no evidence at all of cancer. It was gone. His belly was clear.

I don't believe we really wish cancers upon ourselves. But it does occur to me that perhaps a state of mind can lower or even paralyze one's immunological system. How we feel certainly affects the adrenals and other

glandular output, which in turn affects all other physio-
logical systems. Can't the immunological system be sup-
pressed and even destroyed and also resuscitated in the
same way?

In any case, I found a baby lion head dead, floating on
the surface of the tank today. I bought him in that same
downtown store where I periodically buy small fish
which look good but then never make it into adulthood.
Perhaps there's something about the chemistry of the water in that store that reduces their resistance to illness.
But I never saw a dead fish there. That always happens
later on in my tank.

REFLECTIONS IN A GOLDFISH TANK

A very depressed man came to see me in a consultation today. He knew he was depressed, but he doesn't know what or how much in himself he is depressing and that there is much of his depression which he refuses to allow himself to experience consciously and to accept. Depression is like any other feeling, mood or aspect of ourselves. The more we fight it, the more we deny it, and the more we refuse to allow it full emergence, the longer it hangs on, unable to live itself out and to dissipate. This man has been depressed before and has been afraid of getting depressed again and now he is terrified because he is depressed again.

Though it is very difficult, I now know that the thing is not to be terrified of anything that goes on in us—feeling, thought, mood, fantasy, dream, depression, etc. Through our fear we make it sacred. We hold it at a distance—away from us. Our total concentration and energy are spent outdistancing it and thus our entire beings are inevitably influenced and indeed permeated by it. If we accept it—more than that—if we absorb it openly and fully, we then dilute it with the rest of ourselves and its power is diluted. If we allow ourselves to experience a depression fully, it dissipates quickly and whatever it is that we are depressing or repressing and attempting to keep from ourselves comes up into full awareness. Then we can cope with it and honestly resolve the issues which made for depression in the first place. This, too, is the work of psychoanalysis.

47

Sam is over on his side. He may be suffering from swim-bladder trouble. I think their swim bladders are overtaxed mostly because their odd shapes do not make for stability. Breeding for blimp shapes and long fins has made for a poorly placed center of gravity. If the bladder is affected they never regain their balance for very long. They sometimes right themselves but only for a short time. It's pathetic to see them swim on their backs, over on their sides and on their heads. Some, but only very few, die within a few days. They float on their sides and soon die. Most linger for a long time. I've had fish swim lopsided like that who went right on eating and managing to live for six months or more. But they inevitably succumb to it, either getting more and more crippled so that they can't eat or they go on to develop body ulcers. I think that what kills most of them are damaged or even collapsed lungs. The fish condition like the human condition has its great limitations.

I drained off a third of the bottom water, applied the accessory diatom filter to take out any bacteria, replaced the water with fresh water and put in some kosher salt.

There are two big schools of thought on replacing water and salt. One is pro, one is con. The pro group says that all fish like brackish water. They also say that it's necessary to get rid of urine which accumulates on the bottom of the tank. Fresh water contains traces of chlorine, and this is supposed to be a good antiseptic. The con group says that goldfish don't like salt, too hard to breathe, and that chlorine is a killer. I've tried both and neither seems to matter. When a fish gets sick I always change some water and add salt from time to time, mostly I think because there's nothing else to do. Helplessness and doing nothing is still hard for me to accept. Just waiting is in a way doing something, but it doesn't feel that way to me and I doubt that it does for most people of our country and culture.

Despite the salt and water change, Sam looks the same. He's still over on his side. I care about him very much, but am already reconciled to the worst. This comes from the habit of years of losing fish. Truth is, Sam is one of two fish in the tank I care most about currently. I suppose this is largely so because I've had them both for a long time. The others are relatively new. Why do I call Sam "Sam"? Reminds me of Sam Land? But Land was not a real survivor. He was more of a hanger-on to life. His more prosaic friends really survived, I know now. Sam's time may be up, too. He also reminds me of a fish I had as a child. He was small but round—fat. He was kept in a bowl on a high dresser. One day my mother found him on the floor. He looked dead. In his exuberance he had jumped out of the bowl. Maybe his world was too small for him. He looked battered. Dirt from the floor was embedded in his scales. I put him back in the bowl. He sank to the bottom and looked lifeless. I put some salt in and he seemed to come to life. Eventually he recovered completely and lived for several months. All of us thought it was miraculous. The salt treatment hasn't changed except in those days I used table salt. Anyway I suppose I admire Sam's ability to have lived the few years I've had him, but here he is now, sick. It's also because he's such a lively character. Even now he goes right on looking for food.

I saw a man today in a consultation who in many ways is like my patient Nathan. He told me has has always had a fear of winding up as a bowery bum. He's close to it now. He walked out of his marriage, his job, relationships on all levels. He's learned to drink heavily, too. I say learned because prior to a few years ago he showed no great affinity for alcohol. Interestingly, he did not seem depressed. Then why did he come to see me, I asked? What became evident in our conversation was a powerful detachment. Despite outward behavior otherwise, the man described having always been emotionally detached from everything and everyone. His marriage, his work, his friends—these all represented attempts to satisfy conventional demands. Actually, he resented all of them and this resentment continued even though he managed to stay aloof from involvement despite superficial gestures to the contrary. Now that he has escaped the gestures, too—no job, no marriage, no friends—he is obviously relieved. Then why did he want a consultation with me, I asked again. "Only because of the fear of winding up on the bowery," he told me. Freud said that every fear contains a hidden wish. When I continued to question him it became evident that he strongly desired to be a bowery bum. This would represent the ultimate in freedom from involvement, and this powerful desire terrified him because he is also a rather conventional man after all.

Theodore Isaac Rubin, M.D.

Robert has been in treatment with me for several months. How do I see him? Big, awkward, socially backward—more like a fifteen-year-old than thirty-four, sensitive, serious, very intelligent, fair sense of humor, pleasant looking, very self-effacing, and a genuinely caring person, too, wanting a girl for closeness and to whom to give a considerable storehouse of accumulated affection. He's the antithesis of the "smooth operator," "man about town," "sexual athlete and scorer," shallow and superficial liver, and articulate charmer who is generally thought of as "a lady's man."

Some of his more experienced "friends" have been trying to school him in techniques with women, in making small talk, in being a kind of comic in ways to charm them, intrigue them, induce and seduce them. I can't think of a student who has poorer proclivities in this direction.

I told him that I saw him as a very serious, sensitive man who likes a genuine exchange of information and feelings, too, and who would much prefer silence and silent communication—observing, rather than small talk. I said that I could not see him as a comic. He said that he was enormously relieved to hear this because the attempt to play a role, and he is a very poor actor, is producing increasing inhibition to the point of paralysis. The whole business of a date has come to invoke dread anticipation of performance. The idea that he could drop this and "just be" is enormously relieving, and he said, immediately renews his interest in "getting to know someone."

But he was concerned about "the gawky feel" of him-self—his awkwardness. I explained as best I could that his awkwardness has great grace to it because it is real and that its genuine quality contributes to his consider-able dignity and that the serious person, man or woman, would find his very awkwardness attractive. Any synthet-ic act, especially that of shallow jokester, destroys dignity and destroys the possibility of deep attraction, let alone exchange.

I felt we accomplished something, but not enough. I would have liked to get it across to him—on a gut level—that the thing is not to get rid of the awkwardness—not to get rid of anything. We can't get rid of anything. The idea is to step into it—to step right into the middle of it—to bring one's self smack into the middle of that which we hate about ourselves—to surrender to it and more, to em-brace it, that's not enough, but also to have it embrace us—to envelop us—to be one with it—to add ourselves to it and to be ourselves and even this doesn't say it. But in time I'll get this across to him.

Theodore Isaac Rubin, M.D.

I saw Jack Kearn in his insurance office today to see if the policy on the boat had come in. He said there was nothing doing. I watched Jack. He walks up and down the small village store, sits for a while, walks some more and like the fish in my tank, goes nowhere.

Whenever I see him, he manages to get around to tell me of all the places he's been, lived in, too, and the people he's known. The places include Biarritz, Klosters, Mégève, Paris, Tunis, and a host of others at least equally chic and exotic. Then he tells me of great and well-known musicians, actors, artists, and very successful businessmen and great beauties, too, all former friends and associates. He goes on this way a while and as he does his face lights up and then it seems he catches himself and demeans the past and all the people he knew in that, the glamorous time of his life. Then he tells me how much he likes—no, more than likes, *loves* this little seaside village. No more crowded airports, he tells me, no more traffic, crowds of people, smoke, noise. Now it's all wonderful clean air, quiet and peaceful. He goes into the city every few weeks, and it's enough, more than enough. He looks back "now and then" and can't see what he ever saw in those "so-called great places" or "really boring, pretentious people." He tells me that this place of his feels right, "like an old bathrobe," and he wishes he discovered it and settled down in it years earlier. Now he's convinced it would have added years to his life. I look at him, and he looks robust and healthy and at least ten

54

years younger than his fifty-odd years of age. I look at his office. It's a small room, simple, more than simple—beat up looking, shabby. Perhaps he sees me looking. He tells me that this village, this place is more than good and that he's more than happy. Divorced and through with women, he says he no longer has to look for girls and there's really no point in traveling anyplace anymore. I had the notion that he felt safe here, that he's frightened, that somewhere he got very frightened. When did it happen? Where? How? Is it age? He goes on and tells me of schemes to improve the village—a small museum of old village memorabilia, flower beds, and a restoration of an old village community. But his fright carries through for me, and that's all I see now. I think of the other beach and resort communities I've known in the past. They always seemed to have drawn hurt people, people suffering from more than usual hopelessness. Maybe being at the ocean gives the illusion of being on the edge of the world and as close as one can get to feeling outside of it without surrendering to psychosis. I think of myself, our living room in the New York house—one small corner—the wall is brick—I sit there and it feels cozy and safe. Sometimes I feel that I can sit there forever, and I get up as if attacked and get out and walk to the toughest and most unfamiliar parts of the city. Why? To chance death? Stimulation through taking risks? No, it's to run from that coziness. Kearn is trying to resign, to let go, to surrender. He's found his brick corner, and he's trying but he can't do it. There's a Kearn in Kearn who won't have it these days it wouldn't surprise me at all to hear that he's in Biarritz or Klosters or Mégève again or just generally on the move.

Sam rights himself for a few hours, and then he's on his side again.

The thing about goldfish is that they enable me to sit and stare and do absolutely nothing. This is a sort of long meditating, a real rest, a kind of free-floating mood I get into with them. Perhaps the Japanese and Chinese who've kept goldfish for years used them instead of an internalized mantra. Perhaps I've been doing that these many years. Maybe they are my zen garden. I just know that after an hour of sitting and being with them only, I never fail to feel better, refreshed. For many years a sick fish made this impossible. The quiet balance was disturbed. Instead of the peaceful drifting I would find myself concentrating on the sick fish. But now it's different. Even Sam swimming on his side struggling to right himself doesn't spoil it. Have I become more detached with the years or has my reverie state become more accessible, easier to achieve with habit? Maybe imperfections are no longer felt as discordant. Perhaps it's because I see the entire world more realistically and have more and more given up ideas of utopian perfection and am no longer jarred by sickness being there in the middle of beauty.

Theodore Isaac Rubin, M.D.

This concern about what people think about us and what they say about us runs rampant. This despite self-examination, which almost invariably indicates that we think mostly about ourselves. This ought to be some kind of proof that other people don't sustain much concern or thought about people other than themselves for very long. But this kind of rationale doesn't seem to help at all. The disease continues, and surely it is a disease in its destructive effects. It destroys the feeling of self and self-autonomy, and more than anything it constricts and destroys spontaneity. It's a terrible thing, this concern, and yet it is nearly universal. In a way it even continues after death. I've heard a number of people express concern with how people will feel about them after they are gone. Is it pride? If so, then we actually must feel that pride outlives self. But it's also a projective device designed to rid ourselves of responsibility. It's as if the onus for happiness or sadness, the good or bad decisions we make, are too much to take and we have to see it all in terms of other people. What a loss this represents—this awful need to give up self and to put it into other peoples' hands, people who don't really care because they are engaged in the same process.

Reflections in a Goldfish Tank

Tony, the man I buy most of my goldfish from, periodically reminds me and himself that he never went past the third grade of elementary school. He tells me that in view of his almost complete lack of education he has done extremely well. He goes on to describe an excellent income, a very pleasant life at home including a nice wife and "good kids," two cars, his own house and a boat, too. He loves to go fishing, takes time to do it and likes to eat fish, too. None of this seems to be a defense of any kind, more like a reminder of how well he's doing and he does seem genuinely pleased with himself. He also tells me that he is one of those blessed, rare people who is in a business which purely involves giving people genuine pleasure. All this on a third grade education, he reminds me again, and never once has he theorized what he would have been or done with more education.

Pride is the big killer, the malignant self-digester and Tony's self-reminder of a very limited education seems to be an effective antidote to this most virulent of human poisons. I can't help think of the many people I know with advanced degrees and the superhuman expectations they have of themselves. So many have told me in so many words of what they should have accomplished in view of their educations. What a tragedy that such good stuff should be turned to the service of awful poison.

Today I met a young man at Tony's who works for the sanitation department and seems to know much more about fish illnesses than I do. He felt that there may still be time to save Sam. I may have very well mis-diagnosed his illness. This man says that relatively few fish develop primary or real swim-bladder trouble, and it's much more likely a case of indigestion. He asked if Sam's stools floated and I said they did on occasion. He told me that this is a certain sign of intestinal gas and that gas in a fish makes it impossible for him to swim right side up let alone on a reasonably even keel. He went on to say that Sam might have a chance because he still hasn't been swimming upside down. If he does that for a length of time the condition has become irreversible and the organs are usually affected fatally by this malposition. The cure: no food for three days and then feeding with live food—Daphnia or Tubifex worms for a few weeks. These tiny organisms are more natural foods for goldfish and are apparently more easily digested than dried foods. I thanked him and am already in the process of starving Sam. I hope it works.

Reflections in a Goldfish Tank

Paradox? To him it seemed that way.

He told me of his constriction, detachment and cynicism all of his life. He said that now, suddenly, it all had changed. It was mostly his wife. He didn't care how or why, just that it happened and that's what mattered. He felt more sympathetic and empathetic with people than ever before. More than that, he actually felt warm, open and giving. It was different, different from anything he ever imagined. Now, after twelve years of marriage he and his wife were closer than ever—more than that—they were really close for the first time. He loved her, he "sort of always knew that," but now he felt it. They both felt it, and it felt wonderful for them both and in the middle of all this contentment he met another woman and he likes her, too. More than that, he's infatuated with her. He loves being with her. "Why?" he asked me, "why?" when now for the first time he and wife are feeling "so great together?" "What am I looking for?" he asked. "I have everything I need now—what can I be looking for?"

I explained that people aren't always looking to get something. Sometimes, they look in order to give. Sometimes there is such an abundance of feelings, such an overflow that they feel that they need more than one person to give them to. It's as if they feel that one person won't be able to handle it all and at least another or even more people are needed to receive it all. I said that this is especially true of people who were unused to feeling so much. When they are finally in touch with all that they feel, they find themselves flooded. He understood but

61

still felt that it was "kind of funny" because here it was his wife who finally "reached" him and as a a result he needed his wife and still someone else to deal with what she alone helped generate in the first place.

I explained that another way to put it was that sometimes an initial relationship is so good that it opens people up to wanting more relationships. This went on to a discussion of how some men go for other women out of a sense of deprivation and vindictive rage, while others do it out of openness with that woman and therefore new found love of other women.

We then went on to talk about the attraction of unfamiliarity and how familiar relationships lose the spark of unfamiliar ones. I told him that this largely had to do with the excitement of new beginnings versus the stable commonplace feeling associated with continuing relationships. Some people are attracted to the in-depth "continuings" in which more and more is felt and communicated with each other. Others are attracted to "beginnings"—to the flash feeling of initial encounter and mutual attraction and acceptance. And some people are attracted to both. He said that he felt that he currently fit this latter category. He told me that his new relationship would probably end very soon because of the woman's home circumstances. I said that perhaps in this way it will have served its purpose as a "beginning" relationship and will have ended before it outlived its purpose. He said that he wondered if he would seek out more "beginnings" as the continuing at home became deeper and he felt more and more.

REFLECTIONS IN A GOLDFISH TANK

It's very windy out today. Walking on Third Avenue a few hours ago, I saw a man trying to hold on to his hat, but the wind blew it off anyway. As he went chasing it he held on to his hair, and then I realized it wasn't his hair at all. It was a wig, and the wind took that, too, and then I guess out of force of habit he still held on to his head as he ran to retrieve both his wig and his hat. It was as if the various layers of himself were blowing off. He finally got them both and put them back together on his head as best he could. This time he held the hat down over the wig with a hand on each side, and it looked as if he was holding his real self down so that it could in no way force itself up to the surface and blow away, too. Of course what immediately came to me is how all of us do just that with the layers of embroidery we accumulate along the way to

63

keep our real feelings down and out. But sometimes some of us are lucky enough to get freed for a while by an emotional gust which comes along and blows away our defenses so that we can have a real look at our real selves. Some of us even continue to look and to feel and to be alive even after the wind has died down. I suppose this is another way of looking at what psychoanalysis is supposed to do.

I was buttering a bagel a little at a time, and it occurred to me that the first sign of my father becoming resigned was the way he changed buttering his bread. Changing seemingly unimportant but lifelong rituals may be clues to very deep inner changes.

My father loved bread and used to go to all parts of the city to buy exactly the bread he wanted. Though he was a considerable Talmudic scholar, he was not at all religious and I clearly remember our expeditions to Italian neighborhoods to buy bread during the Passover holiday when the Jewish bakeries were closed.

My father was a very thin man all of his life and this despite the fact that he ate at least the equivalent of a regular-sized loaf of bread a day. His taste included Jewish rye, Italian, small Stumer's pumpernickels and in later years, Pechter's pumpernickel and pieces of heavy Russian black bread cut from huge oblong loaves. He visited us when I was a student in Switzerland, and I think the thing that impressed him most about the country was the fine demi-blanc Swiss bread. He never ate rolls, bagels or cakelike breads and had real contempt for highly refined white breads. He felt quite literally that bread was the staff of life, and he lived in excellent health to eighty-four to prove it. Looking back now, I realize that he ate very little meat and didn't like fancy cooking of any kind. Mostly it was onions, tomatoes, herring, kasha, hot cereals, potato soup, borscht, sour cream, and bread and butter. He didn't at all subscribe to the theory of cholesterol in butter and sour cream being unhealthy.

My father was in total control of bread-cutting at the table, and we asked him for each piece as we wanted it. Slicing the bread in advance either in the bakery or at home was an absolute taboo. He always cut pieces from the loaf as each of us needed it, and he'd butter his own piece a little at a time as he ate it. His method never varied. He cut the bread in irregular chunks holding the loaf against his chest with his left hand and cutting toward himself with his right hand. This using one's chest as a bread board could be dangerous in less experienced hands. Though there was no history of starvation in his background, I remember him getting absolutely frantic whenever there was less than a few loaves of bread in the house.

That this frantic reaction to low bread supply disappeared when he reached eighty, should have given me a clue. A few years later, he seemed to have lost interest in searching out fine bakeries and about a year before he died he just didn't bother anymore with anything other than Jewish rye. But the new way he prepared and buttered his bread was the real giveaway. Unlike all the past years, now before each meal he cut off the several slices of bread he would eat during the meal and then pushed the main loaf away. He then buttered all the slices before he ate, amply indicating that he was no longer interested in the process of cutting each slice off as he needed it and buttering a little piece of the slice at a time as he ate it. What was worse, he no longer took pleasure in cutting bread for anyone else and for the first time each of us cut our own piece off the main loaf. The whole process deteriorated from an intensely pleasurable and involved one to a utilitarian function, and I knew that he had become resigned. He died soon after, and it would be a strange thing to people who don't know, to hear of my sadness when my mother now buys pre-sliced breads.

REFLECTIONS IN A GOLDFISH TANK

I reread the last thing I wrote the other day, and it reminds me of how long fish can go without eating anything at all. This is especially true if they are kept in the dark. Perhaps the lack of light slows their metabolism. Maybe it puts them to sleep. I have noticed that they slow their movements considerably in a semidark room and almost surrender their incessant search for food. I don't remember where I learned this bit of information, but it's a handy thing to know because I've used it whenever we've gone away for three or four days. I just darken the room and they don't seem affected at all by lack of food when I get back. Is this what deadening of feelings is like—a slowup of emotional metabolism, a self-protecting device through a self-imposed state of limbo? Some chronically emotionally deadened people don't seem to age at all. Their faces remain smooth and ageless and their general demeanor reflects little or no emotional experience or impact. I've tried an electric automatic feeder, but this kind of gadget is not quite perfected yet, and it sprays more food out of the tank than into it. Also, the portions it dishes out are too small. It was designed to feed tropical fish, and they eat much less than goldfish.

I remember when I was a child, leaving a neighbor to feed the fish when we went away for a week. All of the fish were bloated and dead when we got back and there were little plants sprouting from seeds contained in the food which had become lodged in the gravel. There was loads of food floating in the tank, and our neighbor ap-

67

parently kept on feeding the tank even after the fish were dead.

This somehow reminds me of overprotecting and stuffing children with too many goodies and how it kills off initiative and spontaneity and ultimately has a stultifying and constricting effect. I've seldom met people who were more psychologically stunted than those who were overprotected as children.

I recently heard that slowly dissolving cubes of food are now available. The fish pick on them as they need them and they last as long as two weeks. Perhaps I'll try them—while I'm here, and if they work I'll use them when we go away.

REFLECTIONS IN A GOLDFISH TANK

I still recall the terrible accident I had with the tank two years ago. The thermostat in the heater went wrong during the night and overheated the water killing all of the fish except one, a chocolate oranda. At first it didn't look as if he would survive either. He developed cataracts over both eyes and had white burn marks over his body and tail. He was actually a barely alive, almost boiled fish. But he survived and that's the way I think of him now, as the survivor. In about three weeks the burn marks disappeared and in three months the cataracts were gone, too. Now there is no evidence at all of what he had been through. He's just a normal-looking medium-sized chocolate oranda. During the time of his healing, he never demonstrated any change of behavior. Despite obvious blindness during that period, he managed to find all the food he needed, indeed he never stopped eating, and this is perhaps the main thing about him. I bought Sam after I was sure the survivor was all better. I didn't want him to have to compete for food. During the last year and a half I've added the others, but as I said earlier, I'm most attached to these two.

No fish eats like the survivor, not even Sam, who is twice his size, even when he, Sam, is in the best of health. The survivor gobbles up at least half the food before the other fish even realize that it is there. Between feedings he continuously dives into the gravel looking for stray crumbs. The others go over the gravel, pick up a little at a time, strain it and puff it out, hardly making any impact at all. The survivor actually dives from about a foot up off

69

the bottom of the tank, head first into the gravel, repeatedly and therefore does find food buried deeper than the surface grains. I've never seen a fish do this and I've never seen one with equal zeal and energy. As I write now I can actually hear him banging against the gravel. He doesn't get bloated or fat, and I suppose this is mainly due to his constant activity.

This zeal to live, this enormous vitality, the survivor has it, the other fish don't, at least not the special kind of life affirmation that he has. Is it an inborn thing? Does it apply to people? I believe that our species has come a long way, that we have evolved beyond instincts and their dictates, that we are capable of free choice. I also believe that emotional damage early in life can destroy vitality and that neurotic depression can create a hopelessness and despair which surely can cripple the desire to survive. But I have met people, especially of my father's generation, whose zeal to live seemed to come from their very substance and I wonder if this zeal to live isn't an inborn core, organic, thing, which is either there or not right from the start.

REFLECTIONS IN A GOLDFISH TANK

Betty, a woman we know from the beach, called me last night. She was in the city for a few days, and she suddenly had an attack of terrible panic. She said that the city always depresses her, this despite the fact that she loves it. When I asked her to elaborate, she said that she loved the aliveness and vitality, but this was the very thing that throws her into a panic. "Everyone seems goal-directed, busy, doing things and by comparison I feel worthless, disorganized, nothing to accomplish, inept." She said that this never happens at the beach. "I feel safe there, no one else is doing anything either. Nothing is expected of me."

Safe from what, from her self-hating attacks, punishment from self-imposed exorbitant expectations of self? I strongly suspect that while relatively few people live at the beach all year round, most of them are there for the same reason—to escape. Escape what, their own terrible drives, expectations, attacks on self for seeming failures? How about those of us who go there on weekends or for vacations? Do we go for the same reason or is it really to escape external pressures or both?

Theodore Isaac Rubin, M.D.

We psychoanalysts are the detectives, the real detectives. What other detective spends his entire working day putting together people's free associations—seemingly meaningless disconnected thoughts and making sense out of them? No, it's more than sense we make out of them—*sense* connotes logic, and logic and intellectual insight are meager goals in this activity. We put it all together, we probe, we ask for more associations to associations, and we keep putting more and more together to discern feelings, to get at what people really feel. Yes, this is where we are at in our species' cultural evolution. The more than last hundred thousands years have brought us to a point where we have covered up what we feel with so much defensive embroidery that we need each other to tell each other what it is we really feel. We, the analysts, are the professionals at this peculiar and highly contrived activity. Someone comes in, sits up or lies down, talks and talks some more, and the other person tells him or her what he or she is *really saying* on a feeling level. So there we are all day—each of us in this odd profession—listening to person after person and deciphering, decoding and helping to open up one's feelings, that is, to get by the censor of acculturated niceties, and it works and it's also such hard work. This business of deciphering feelings is no intellectual game for the analyst either. He must use his own associations and associative memories and experiences and feelings to feel out what it is his patient is feeling. Yes, he, the total detective analyst is the best and only instrument he has in this strange game—a game in which two people are really trying to dilute and mitigate the poisons secondary to culture and civilization. So what we do all day is to try to extend aliveness and spontaneity and to feel who we are when we are our own special alive selves. I say *we* because if the analyst doesn't grow, too, then we can be sure that nothing worthwhile is happening, because this kind of mutuality is characteristic of this kind of human struggle and there is no getting around it. Therefore, the analyst must go through this growing experience all day, day after day, and it's no wonder at all that we who are engaged in this peculiar work are so tired by the end of the day.

Theodore Isaac Rubin, M.D.

I've tried the young sanitation man's treatment (the man I met at Tony's) several times. I starved Sam for twenty-four hours, and then I fed him Tubifex worms four times with several days between treatments. It hasn't helped. He's still over on his side so I guess he's not suffering from excess gas caused by indigestion. My original diagnosis of swim-bladder trouble must be correct after all. Another man I met at Tony's place says that he heard that swim-bladder trouble is a congenital defect that shows up when a fish is between two or three years of age. I've also heard that it's the result of radical changes in water temperature, changes in atmospheric pressure and is a kind of "bends" produced by a faulty chemical balance in the blood stream. Nobody seems to know, and this reminds me of the various human diseases of unknown etiology—diabetes, multiple sclerosis, psoriasis, pemphigus, neoplasms, schizophrenia, and I'm sorry to say that the list goes on and on. The last one, schizophrenia, I feel more and more is probably not one illness at all, but rather a group of symptoms with many different causes in different human beings. Perhaps this is also true of fish who cannot maintain their physical equilibrium in the water. Maybe the causes are multiple and different in each case. Who knows—perhaps they are even emotional—to what extent do creatures of other species suffer from emotional disturbances? Primates and dogs do and psychologists claim that dogs' neurotic problems stem largely from identification with people. We really know so little about the emotional lives of other species—

indeed in most cases, nearly all, we don't really know if they have emotional lives at all. But for that matter, we are surely only beginning to scratch the surface of insight into the emotional workings and psychodynamics of our own species. In any case, the fish I call Sam is still mostly swimming about unbalanced—slightly upended and on his right side.

T oday I am fifty-three years old and the day after to-morrow Ellie will be fifty-one.

The illusions I've had about aging are no different from any of the others. What I mean is, that they were always just as unrealistic but like the others, of course, I didn't know this until confrontation with reality was forced upon me. In this case, getting older is the reality. Some-how I had the idea that one is suddenly old and then suddenly still older and so on. I really didn't see it as an evolving process at all. For example, I knew in my head, but not at all in my feelings, that real physical changes and emotional ones, too, take place and keep taking place. These include easy fatigability and equal loss of ease in falling asleep, especially when sleep is interrupted; moodiness and greater difficulty in willfully changing moods; greater need to urinate—more frequency and urgency and lesser ability to urinate with youthful vigor and pressure; good appetite and poor ability to digest all kinds of foods; more understanding and more irritability, too, and on and on this list goes. And it comprises, I realize now, the not-so-simple process of aging, which is really not so bad except for the shock when it comes up against the gut expectation to have no increase in aches and pains, but just a totally graceful easing into being a gracious older and still older person.

And then I look at myself. I hardly see a change at all. But then I look at my children and I know I've changed because they look like someone I knew thirty years earlier when I looked in the mirror and except for a vague family resemblance, they don't look like me now. And I look at Ellie and she at me and in our minds' eye we see each other as we were then and we know we've gotten older—much older and we kiss and hug each other and this helps make a deeply felt pain in the heart go away as the pictures of ourselves in our youth mercifully fade away, too.

REFLECTIONS IN A GOLDFISH TANK

Perhaps the most difficult part of having a sick fish in the tank is my reluctance to put any new fish in there with him. I wrote reluctance, actually it's prudence, but it is frustrating because one of my big joys is to buy a new fish now and then. Like any grown-up child, I don't take frustration all that well. Yet, why not put new fish in? This swim-bladder trouble is in no way contagious and yet this is a kind of prudent taboo inasmuch as I almost never really have a true and definite diagnosis with these goldfish of mine. Also, seeing a very expensive fish sick often discourages me to the point where I'm ready to give up the whole thing and am certainly in no mood to buy new fish. What I realize thinking and feeling about this now is that I'm angry with Sam. He can't help his sickness but neither can I help my anger at him for being sick and causing me irritation. More than irritation—anger, inconvenience and also spoiling a good mood. A large fish lingering that way, and he may linger for months, is certainly not uplifting. Now how much of this kind of feeling is mixed in with true empathy, sympathy, caring, love and pain when people are involved? All of it I'm sure and I'm also sure that it causes us a great deal of misery—not because it's there, but because we won't accept these "negative" feelings about sickness in our midst on a conscious level where we can handle them. Instead, we repress them and pose as other than we are as reverberations from down below come up to make us confused, depressed and often physically sick, too.

77

Theodore Isaac Rubin, M.D.

Well, I love Sam, but I'm also fully aware that I'd like him to either get well or disappear.

A nephew of mine, by marriage, visited me today. This was strange because I hardly ever see him, and we have remarkably little in common. At first, I couldn't make out what the visit was all about. It seemed from the moment he walked in that it did have a purpose. More than that, I could tell that he had a singular purpose in mind, but what? Throughout the beginning of his arrival I noticed that he had a kind of swagger, that he came on stronger than when I had seen him in the past. But I also picked up more than usual restless movement, some sweating and teeth clenching. I could tell that despite the swagger, he was more anxious than usual, actually quite tense. I wondered if he came to tell me of an emotional problem

78

or perhaps for a referral to another doctor. But then he told me, and this was immediately followed by a noticeable easing up. He told me that he had landed a big, prestigious, lucrative job with a well-known firm on the West Coast. He had "finally made it. I am finally a success."

Now why did he come to tell me and why the swagger? Some kind of paternal transference to me? No, he has parents of his own and seems to be on good terms with them. Also, interestingly, he's not that much younger than me. But after he left and I went over the visit, I realized what this was about. I remembered how well he scrutinized my face and watched my reaction after he told me "the news." I remembered how relieved he seemed and how relaxed he was when he left except for the swagger. The anxiety seemed to be gone, but the swagger was even more exaggerated than when he arrived. I'm sure that he has no conscious idea at all why he came to tell me his big news, but I feel I know. How harsh our culture continues to be.

Being "very successful," and I know through easy accessibility to the family grapevine, I've been touted as such, is like being a gun fighter. In our extended family, I have inadvertently been dubbed the "fastest gun in town." Therefore, I am the one to challenge, the one to come up against, the one to beat. As the "big gun," some younger people come to ask favors, others to emulate, others to depend on and some to measure against and to put down and surpass. The last is characteristic of the proud ones, my nephew. I realize now, why he always begged off visits to our house. He had to wait until he was "ready" and then he came.

T oday I heard myself saying, to a man who came to see me for a consultation, "that the battle is half won once a person can see himself as a 'patient' and come for help."

Is this just another rote and foolish cliché? It is true that motivation is all important and now after a good many years in practice I feel fairly certain that nobody can be sales-talked into being motivated to get help. So what is this all about? Having motivation seems more related to pain than to insight. The only insight most people have when they start treatment is the awareness of suffering, and the awareness that they want relief. Sometimes they are also aware that current painful difficulties like severe depression are related to long-standing deeper problems.

But, half the battle *is* really won—why? Motivation, yes! But it's more than that. What I think it really amounts to is that having "symptoms and emotional pain" strong enough to be motivated to come for help, is evidence of winning the battle against resignation, hopelessness, and the illusion that all is well. This "allowing oneself" to "come apart" enough to feel pain so as to need help, is, I suspect, a kind of unconscious decision which separates the population into those who will go on frozen in a neurotic status quo and those who will accept sufficient pain and confusion as to help real clarifying to take place. Therefore, half the battle is won when a person comes for help. It's not won because of the help itself, but because coming for help is symbolic of the fact that half the battle has already been won in deciding to let go enough to get out of the neurotic freeze.

Theodore Isaac Rubin, M.D.

Today I decided to stand up against illogic. I bought a medium-sized calico oranda, and it gave me a lot of pleasure. This despite the fact that Sam is still over to one side. I notice how most people are rather careless about how they choose the fish they buy. They buy according to what attracts them, to what they like. But they pay virtually no attention to the fish's state of health.

One must watch and see that they swim properly, eat heartily, have no small ich spores anywhere on them, no bubblelike little worms especially in the tails, no fungus, no cut or missing fins, no body sores, (especially on the pedicle to which the tail is attached), and no predilection to attack other fish. A mixture of dilute metholine blue and methiolate painted on a sore combined with tetracycline in the water sometimes cures body sores. But more often, sick fish go on and die despite heroic treatment. Also, their eyes should be clear, no cataracts, and in orandas it is important to make sure that the lion head hood does not cover mouth, eyes or gills. I'm careful about all this, and I still bring home sick fish on occasion. Tony is very good about this and accepts returns, but other fish stores are adamant on this point. Once a fish leaves the store, it is no longer theirs.

When I first started with goldfish and a fairly big tank and began to buy fancy ones, I put both plants and rocks in the water. They always dig up the plants and often cut themselves on rocks. If they wedge themselves between rocks they will not back out but will attempt to squeeze their way through even if this is impossible. Either they completely lack judgment in this regard, are self-destructive or just plain stubborn. If no one is there to back them out, they will struggle to get through for hours, to the point of completely destroying themselves. This is not unlike members of our own species who so often refuse to extricate themselves from impossible situations. In any case, goldfish are better off without rocks or ornaments and they uproot and eat plants. They do best in plain, clear, aerated, well-filtered water with an inch of gravel on the bottom. Some people add kosher salt and some don't. I don't. I no longer feel that it helps in any way and it precipitates out all over the top of the tank and requires constant cleaning. Speaking of tanks. Plexiglass tanks leak much less frequently and are lighter to handle but they scratch easily. Gravel of greater depth buries food which rots and clouds the water. Goldfish eat and excrete a great deal therefore it is a good idea to clean filters often and to change a third of the water, bottom water if possible, every few weeks. Goldfish urine is acid and the pH of the water is best kept slightly alkaline. This is easily done with a pH kit and bicarbonate of soda. This is the price or prices to pay for keeping these fish, again, not unlike paying the price required for everything in life.

She told me how she "splurged" and how crazy she felt for doing it. No, more than crazy, guilty too. She felt that it was wrong to spend so much money. It was inconsistent with how she always behaves. It was irrational, and also she couldn't afford it. She went on recriminating this way and then went on to recall and to recount the several times in her life (she is thirty-nine years old) when she acted with "total unpracticability." I told her that they were paltry few and that they all unfortunately lacked the quality of real abandon and foolishness. She said she didn't understand. I told her that most people when they reach the age of eighty or ninety and add it all up, are not at all angry about the irrationalities in their lives, but rather at the multitude of staid, proper, practical rationalities. They are angry and disappointed that there were not nearly enough irrationalities, impracticalities, times of great foolishness, times of acting out with total abandon, times of childish and ridiculous bad judgments and silly and selfish self-indulgences. I told her that compiling a list of these is important for the future and that she was way behind and had better begin at once.

REFLECTIONS IN A GOLDFISH TANK

If I was asked to give only one piece of advice it would again be *not to overfeed them*. I'm convinced that giving them relatively little food, distributed several times over the day is the most important factor in keeping goldfish alive. Too much food kills them. It gluts and bloats them. They become much less active. A kind of listlessness inundates them. I've watched them and they soon develop one or another killing diseases. I've come to believe that they have to have just little enough food to struggle for it. This struggle and activity make for longevity.

These fish eat all the time. I'm certain that in a natural habitat, nearly all their lives are spent looking for food with only minimal success. Provide maximum success and we destroy their balance and their very being. Maybe this is pure magic, but watching them, I have the feeling that lacking the struggle destroys their inner identity. They no longer know who they are and they develop a kind of hopelessness which leads to death.

I'm immediately reminded of this very expensive apartment building some people I know live in. They've had roof pool parties that I've attended a number of times over the years. I've gotten to know some of the people there. There are several who confided in me immediately and then went on telling me about themselves each time I saw them. They are nearly all children of extremely wealthy people. But the unique thing about the people of this building is that none of them came from people of old wealth. Their parents were the first of their families to make big money and these, their children, were reaping the reward. Interestingly, the highlights of their lives were always described in terms of their parents both in parental struggles and successes. Some of them had only heard about these struggles and others only retained fragments of early memories because these were the only vital, really alive times they connected themselves with at all. There were none in their personal lives and they went on to tell me of their chronic depressions, disappointments, hypochondriasis and various psychosomatic disorders. Each time I've been with these people I've picked up that same kind of lack of raison d'être, the same kind of empty listlessness I see in overfed goldfish. Periodically I've heard about suicides, bad accidents and malignant illnesses among them. It seems paradoxical that their parents struggled at least in some part to provide this East Side Mecca for their children and unwittingly somehow contributed to a stylish habitat and inner deadness. It took me a long time to learn, but I never overfeed my fish anymore.

REFLECTIONS IN A GOLDFISH TANK

I told him that he was a "yearner," and I could tell he didn't know what I meant. I explained that we are all yearners in part, but that some people make yearning the central dynamic of their lives, and I call these people "yearners."

These people live in their imaginations more than other people do. The real world eludes them. Their lives are full of fantasy, and this includes a fantasy value system little or none of which exists on a reality level. Theirs is often a Shangri-la world populated by perfect people and a place of constantly interesting high adventure and pure ideals. But the real "yearner" uses yearning as the fuel which feeds the fantasies. He knows "deep down" that his world is in no way actualized and he blames unrequited love, unrequited opportunity, unrequited everything for his inability to bring his imaginary world into actual existence. Eventually *yearning* becomes his sole way of feeling alive. Yearning becomes his reason for living and provides whatever aliveness he feels. Yearning— wanting something he cannot get—provides him with the central core of feeling and energizes his imaginary world. *If* is the big word in yearning and so is *only*. *If only* he could get this or that or *if only* this or that would happen—then *it* would all come true. *But* it is extremely important that he never does get this or that, and that this or that does not happen. Indeed the yearner must be extraordinarily careful to not get whatever it may be he yearns for because this would destroy his yearning and would also destroy his imaginary world. This would precipi-

Theodore Isaac Rubin, M.D.

tously thrust him into the real world of real people and
real values and very real limitations, none of which he is
prepared to cope with. It would also destroy the many
claims for special privilege of all kinds that he has made
on the basis of what he often perceives as unjust unrequited desires. His continuous yearning keeps him in a
state of synthetic suffering and glorious martyrdom and
the abused feelings he suffers keep him feeling alive and
hopeful. The hope lies in the *if* and *but.* Periodically I
have seen yearners who have unwittingly actualized a
yearning they have had and this usually leads to bitter
disappointment, loss of sense of importance and identity
and severe anxiety and depression. The yearner knows
this on an unconscious level and therefore manages to
run out of steam just before the novel is completed, to get
sick just before the contract is signed, to sabotage the relationship which was supposed to be the most desirable,
etc., in order to go on yearning and to maintain the synthetic hope for paradise linked to fulfillment of the yearning, which must of course never take place. My yearning
patient is currently yearning for a relationship with a
woman he sees on the train every day whom he has never
met. Of course he must never meet her, and he spends a
great deal of time avoiding this possibility and at the
same time adding to the highly romantic fantasy of what
an encounter with her would bring to his life. This pseudo-life of his occupies much more time than his real life.
Probing the last few weeks has turned up various yearning preoccupations about people and work, which keep

his pseudo-life active and in control of the major part of his psyche. Last week he went into some detail about the "girl who got away." He knew her for years and "came close" (a typical phrase of yearners) to marrying her, but somehow the "timing was wrong," (typical) and she finally married someone else. He said he felt like saying, "You fool, you threw away our lives," but instead he "wished her luck, felt very sad and just went on living." And yearning, I might add, for what could have been. Yes, the young lady in question actually helped in his construct of the life that could have been and in this way aided his pseudo-life plan.

I explained a bit of this to him and I think he understood. He came up with several associations of how he managed to frustrate himself in a number of activities just in time to save himself from meaningful fruition. But I have no illusions about helping yearners. The job is a long, arduous one. It involves suffering a good deal of anxiety. Surrendering illusions involved in an intricately organized imaginary world brings great pain and a sense of awful impoverishment. This loss, and it is felt as a great loss, must take place slowly and carefully so that the yearner can replace fantasy with gratifications of reality. If no time and practice is devoted to replacement with *real* satisfactions, the ensuing emptiness can lead to overwhelming depression and even suicide. Replacing imaginary cake with real bread is not easy, but it can be done and most yearners know and want this. This is why they come to treatment. Yes, they also come to try to actualize their imaginary lives, but I believe that in the deepest part of themselves their principal motivation is to replace synthetic lives with real living.

I saw a very old lady crossing Third Avenue today against traffic, and she seemed almost totally oblivious to the cars and trucks. I say *seemed* and *almost* because when a few of the cars started honking, she just waved her hand at them to quiet down and kept walking. Now this is a scene I've seen at least a hundred times. Does old age bring with it a kind of ruthless, noncaring arrogance? If it's not caring, is it not caring about one's self or other people or both? If it's arrogance, is the feeling one of special privilege because of age? Is the old lady making the statement—"I've lived in this world a long, long time, and I'm no longer in awe of it or anything in it, including you. Having lived in it so long it owes me a little something extra, and this includes crossing the street regardless of what color the traffic light shows"? Is it a feeling of having little time left to wait or no longer being willing to put up with waiting especially for things like automobiles? Is there anything possibly healthy in the act—a kind of self-assertive defiance, a dropping off of compulsive, compliant niceties, an impatience with superficial cultural artifacts. Could it even be part of a deeper dynamic—a feeling that existence is important but no longer at the cost of dignity—an unwillingness to pay the price of noise, foul air, crowding, etc.—the falling out of love with life at any price—life as it is now? My associations are perhaps leading me to being quite fanciful and unrealistic. They also lead me down still another road. I remember patients who had been hospitalized in state hospitals for many years—entire lifetimes—people who had elaborately constructed deep psychotic psychologies. These people had lived in their own seclusive worlds for forty years or more and a good number of them in reaching their late sixties and early seventies suddenly gave up all of their psychotic elaborations. They stopped hallucinating, stopped their delusional beliefs, gave up their special uncomprehensible language and made real and sustained contact with the rest of the world. Some of the staff said that the psychosis burned off, whatever that really means. It was as if they had enough of the psychotic enterprise. Perhaps they were tired of holding back whatever it was they were running from in the first place. They were sick of the subterfuge

of craziness, and they gave it up and became their real
selves.

Time, he explained to me, is of the essence to him.
Money spent for his treatment doesn't matter at all. He is
ready to pay any fee at all. But time is something else. He
understands that psychoanalytic treatment is a continuing process and requires at least several sessions a week
(three or more is best, we of our analytic school think)
regularly scheduled, but time is too valuable for him. He
just can't take the time to get to my office, and he knows
that our therapeutic relationship and endeavor would not
be well-served for me to come to him. I explained that
motivation was all important and that I could well understand the great value he put on his time. *But,* I asked him,
won't the time to come to his sessions be well spent, inas-

much as this time will be used in behalf of himself? He said he understood, but that it was impossible and then he suggested we use the telephone. I told him that this was a too limited way to communicate. We needed to see each others' faces, hands and movement generally and more than that, to sense each others' presence, for the kind of communication we needed to take place. He said he understood, but I knew he really didn't because he still persisted that he couldn't do it. I also told him that I thought he had established a pride position in his insistence and that from everything he told me, he was used to having his own way. I said that if he had his own way in this issue, he would, in his frame of reference, establish control of the treatment. This I told him would mean that he would have won this initial confrontation with me and would from the beginning doom the success of the treatment. He said he understood and smiled and this I think he did understand as he is used to all kinds of power plays in business deals that he conducts. He then asked if I wouldn't just try it by phone, that maybe I would find out that it would work out after all. I asked, that if it didn't, would he then come to my office for his sessions? He smiled sadly and said, "In all honesty, no, I would not." I said that I didn't think he was ready for treatment—that is, psychoanalytic treatment, and to give me a ring in the future if he changed his mind. We shook hands and as he left he told me that he respected me for my decision. I asked if that meant that he would have disrespected me had I acquiesed to his arrangement? He admitted that he would have and as a matter of fact would have had contempt for me "as just another guy whom he had bought." I told him that it was too bad he had arranged this kind of bind for himself, because it made treatment of this kind impossible for him.

A good night out, an interesting party, some good talk, new people can almost serve as a brief vacation. It can linger on in memory for a while and help dilute some everyday pressures. But what about a bad night out, and is there such a thing and whose responsibility is it?

The other night we went to a restaurant with some friends on Long Island. It was a last-minute thing, and they insisted we come along with them and a group of ten of their neighbors we had never met who had arranged this particular evening several months earlier.

The talk among us couldn't have been more superficial.

REFLECTIONS IN A GOLDFISH TANK

It was as if everyone made a concerted effort not to exchange anything whatsoever about what anybody felt about anything. We usually have much to communicate with these friends of ours, but this time it was as if there was nothing at all to say. Unlike any restaurant I've been in for years, there was a band and people danced. I felt somehow dislocated as if moved back in time some thirty years. One man from a table with other men got up and danced each dance with women from different tables. Their escorts seemed to welcome his invitations to the women they were with. He came close to our table each time around the floor and whispered the exact same words to each woman, nuzzling her neck and cheek. Strangely, each of them seemed flattered and happy with his attentions, even though she just saw him pay exactly the same attentions to the preceding women. The women's husbands, and I think they were husbands, smiled benignly and I think may have been relieved because they didn't have to dance. The evening went like that and it was a long evening, some three and a half hours. The food by the way was only passable. When we finally left we felt exhausted and irritated and this feeling lasted a few days. What went wrong? I'm sure we were as responsible as everyone else. Was it that most of the people were strangers? Did our friends feel constrained among a mixture of their friends—were we strangers among the others? Did the feeling of dislocation affect us so strongly? I usually like meeting new people, but this time I didn't care to find out about them. The highlight of the evening was watching the one man dance seductively with the different women. But this was not enough. Somehow none of us seemed at all inclined to make the necessary effort or emotional or intellectual investment to find out about the others. I wondered if all these neighbors really knew any more about each other than we did. It was more than lack of inclination though. It was inhibition—paralysis—we were all caught in our separate moods of deep apathy and this was the general mood that prevailed. A few weeks later I found out that we all had at least several areas in common, but nobody cared to find that out about them that night at the table. We were somehow all of us determined to ignore each other except for superficial niceties. I guess we were all in the same mood at the same time and none of us could come to our mutual rescue.

REFLECTIONS IN A GOLDFISH TANK

I was at a meeting of the joint management committee of the clinic today. These meetings are rather formal and altogether quite serious. I looked at us and it suddenly struck me that everyone of us was wearing a wristwatch. This suddenly struck me as one of the craziest and funniest scenes I've ever encountered. There we were all these terribly serious, grown-up people, all of us with these little metal mechanisms tied to our wrists. Not only that, but we kept looking at our wrist mechanisms, as I came to call them in that moment, and it was obvious that we were slaves to them. It was as if we were receiving directions from the things tied around our wrists. The scene burst upon me as so inane I couldn't keep from laughing. They wanted to know what I was laughing about but I wouldn't tell them. Each time anyone looked at his wrist I'd start all over again. I could tell by some of the expressions on their faces that they were more annoyed than worried for my sanity. But I felt I couldn't tell them. It was a private joke and telling it would spoil it. Also, how could I tell it? It was one of those rare insights into some of the more ridiculous aspects of our lives that sometimes bursts on you, feelings of which can't really be conveyed. I suspect this particular one is related to a growing inner and mostly unconscious awareness of many of the conforming and conventional rigid uniformities we are all caught in.

97

Theodore Isaac Rubin, M.D.

I wrote about that boring evening of superficial small talk in the restaurant and yet at the same time I must say I also put a certain value on superficiality and shallowness. Sometimes I get so tired of the heavy deep mood so characteristic of my many Russian Jewish relatives. Is this prejudice? Perhaps, in part, it is, and if it is, it is also a form of self-hate because I certainly include myself in the group. But I think more than anything it is a sociocultural affliction. I think we have a tendency to embrace depression in bad times and to sustain a heavy at least moderately sad mood in good times. I remember my father sitting in a dark room, and when I asked him why he didn't turn on the light, telling me that he enjoyed the gloomy feeling the darkness gave him. I also remember the objections and derision some of my relatives felt for a young man a cousin of mine was going with. He was a young lawyer, and he turned out to be a very capable lawyer, but he somehow struck them as being "too light, too shallow, not serious enough." When they found out that he played basketball in his spare time, their worst fears were confirmed. This proved that he was a superficial person and would surely spend the rest of his life as a kind of "empty, nonserious lightweight." Looking back now, I realize that this young man's only fault, as they saw it, was that he seemed fairly happy most of the time and capable of enjoying many things, including some outside the purely intellectual and artistic realm. He just showed no promise at all in his ability to contribute seriously to an air of general gloom. It is interesting how people can arrogate to themselves an absolute certain opinion as to what is good and bad in life, relative to a cultural frame of reference which may be quite aberrated, without any awareness on their part. I guess I'm talking about sick pride—being proud and extolling that which is narrow, constricted and prejudicial. In this case, I feel that the best antidote is at least some small dose of superficiality and shallowness and, above all, fun. I wish it for my children, but I often doubt that we've succeeded because I see them on the "heavy side" too much of the time. I've told them without too much effect that I'd like to see them take some shallowness—seriously.

Theodore Isaac Rubin, M.D.

I was going over some money matters with Ellie a few hours ago and I asked myself if I would write for money. I mean suppose a publisher offered me a great deal of money to write a book. Perhaps, I don't know. I would have to believe in the book. I know that I don't turn down anything I want to write because there may not be any money in it. I write because it makes me feel good to write. Yet, I certainly enjoy what money I get for a book after it's written. More than that—I want it to sell well. I want it to be read and I want it to make money, too. But when I write it, these things are not in mind. They come into being when the process of writing is over. I don't feel particularly virtuous about this and have no contempt whatsoever for people who say they write only for money. I've met people who say they do this, but some of their writing seems to come from a level deeper than practical need and at least in part they may be fooling themselves.

REFLECTIONS IN A GOLDFISH TANK

I took the black glass gravel out of the tank and replaced it with golden glass gravel. I made sure that the gravel had no sharp points, because I could easily imagine the survivor bruising himself in his power dives. As I said earlier, any kind of cuts are disastrous in goldfish. Fungus infections form at once. The black gravel made a dramatic contrast with the red-colored fish, but it also absorbed a great deal of the light. Putting in stronger lights results in fast algae growth so that you can hardly see through the front glass. The golden gravel gives the tank a soft warm hue and plenty of light. Taking gravel out and replacing it in a tank full of water is not easy, but it was worth it.

The new calico oranda is doing just fine. The first few weeks are crucial because they determine whether or not adequate adaptation to a new environment has taken place. It's probably wisest not to buy a fish until the retail fish dealer has had him for several months. This at least indicates an ability to adapt to the store's tank, some of them having come from breeder's ponds. But this means keeping track of a particular fish over a period of time and of course he may be sold in an active store. A deposit on a fish may hold him while his health is tested provided the dealer agrees to this arrangement. Some dealers will do this especially if a fish is more than forty or fifty dollars. Anyway, with the new fish I floated the bag of water he came in so as to equalize the temperature and gradually replaced water in the bag with water from the tank, giving him time to get used to the new water, and

101

then I put him in the tank. The entire transfer took about two hours. Perhaps it was worth it. In any case, the tank is just about perfect, but not quite—Sam is almost constantly over on his side and hardly rights himself at all anymore.

I got a letter from a lady today who read an article I wrote and objected to my repeated use of the word *history*. She said that if I could rid myself completely of male chauvinism, I would at least occasionally say *herstory* instead of *history*. Perhaps she's right.

Thinking about it I realize that in a sense, men and women, or perhaps I should say women and men, have come to represent two different cultures. One is highly competitive, game-oriented, aggressive and prone to war. The other is gentler, warmer, more expressive of feelings, more interested in realistic needs, more involved with children and more pacific.

Of course there is overlapping, too. Perhaps in the future, when women have received all the rights men have, they will be less interested in emulating men and more interested in making contributions and prompting influences of their more mature culture. At that time, perhaps mothers will bring up both sons and daughters not to go to war under any circumstances. I'd like to think that presidents and prime ministers will be women whose prime interest will be peace and who will abhor violence and national self-glorification through military conquest. Should that time arrive—gentler feelings and expressions, love of music, poetry and babies and real respect for people regardless of which sex they are, will be considered neither masculine nor feminine, but just human. Not too long after that time, sick pride, competition, and vindictive triumphs would be a thing of the past.

Theodore Isaac Rubin, M.D.

She asked me what I thought real happiness consisted of. I thought of what I had felt and written about happiness in the past: essentially that happiness is a state of relative well-being rather than a high or series of highs.

But I told her that one kind of very important happiness is communication with another person. Being unable to communicate must surely represent one of the great unhappinesses of the human condition.

I went on to say that real communication sometimes takes place in a flash second with hardly any seeming effort at all. But mostly, this isn't the case. Mostly, it takes place only with a great deal of struggle and commitment. I mean mutual commitment to the desire to help each other understand each other's feelings about the particular subject in question. This almost always involves a lot of struggle, but this is a struggle for happiness. This is so, because with mutual insight comes an indescribable happiness—a kind of peace born of hope for ourselves and the entire species.

REFLECTIONS IN A GOLDFISH TANK

Some years ago, when I went through a very painful depression, I gave away the tank I had at that time, and of course the goldfish in it. What I recall now is how irresistible the urge was. More than irresistible—it was compelling. I felt an enormous pressure to get rid of it all, the tank, the fish and any other equipment, and I couldn't rest until I did. What was this about? Perhaps an act of self-hate or an attempt to rid myself of any responsibility at all or trying to relieve pressure any way at all? I really don't know. Perhaps it was a combination of many things. The one thing that occurs to me now, in thinking about it, which I've not thought about before, is that perhaps I was clearing the way of anything whatsoever that might get in the way of my being depressed. It's as if I wanted to feel the full impact of the depression and wanted nothing to interfere or to dilute it. Also, I was settling down for the long haul—a long, difficult confrontation with myself and with unfinished business. I think now that I knew that this confrontation would take all the time and energy I had, and there would be none left for the fish. They could not, and I did not, want them to depend on me. In any case when I gave them away I was at first particularly hard hit, but soon after felt relieved and did in fact get down to the internal business at hand. Perhaps this was all ceremonial, a symbolic ritual I needed to indicate to myself the seriousness of how badly I felt and the work on myself I needed. I suspect we do, in fact, give ourselves important messages of this kind without awareness of motivation many times in our lives. I did keep a favorite air pump; maybe it represented hope for myself in the future, and I used it a few years later when I reestablished another tank and my depression was finally over.

"If she says 'yes,'" he told me, "it does something for my ego." I told him that I thought that it does nothing at all for his ego, that it in no way strengthens or adds to his ego. What it might do, I said, was to neutralize his lack of ego—to temporarily mitigate his own chronic and constant assault on his ego.

Why do some men chase women? What are sexual conquests really about? Yes, of course there's the physical pleasure, the lust and sometimes love, too. But this doesn't account for the compulsivity involved. I think it's the fear of rejection again. Her sexual acquiesence is felt as the ultimate proof of her acceptance. It's the ultimate anti-rejection tonic and like most tonics, the required dose has to be repeated again and again. Rejection is felt as proof of one's really being no good. It is major fuel for feeding self-hate and self-rejection. Acceptance or what is interpreted as acceptance is felt as the antidote. Sexual acceptance is felt as the big one—the real one—the big cure. In this way we can say that the conquest is an attempt to conquer one's own self-hate. Of course it's covered up with all kinds of pride in one's masculine attributes, but the empty feeling that soon follows, and the compulsion to embark on the quest again and again, is evidence of the underlying truth. So, are these men victims of feelings of their mothers' lack of full acceptance? Is this an unresolved sexual yearning for mothers? Is it looking for mama again and again? Perhaps, and yet there probably is no one answer to any particular form of human behavior. Some people are surely more sensual than others. I think this is even true of goldfish. I have a small lionhead, who goes up and back through the air pump's bubbles turning this way and that. He looks just like anyone who enjoys feeling a strong shower of water on his or her skin. He's the only one of my fish who does this, and perhaps it's fanciful, but I think he feels and enjoys much. Some men play out a hostile, sadistic love-them-and-leave-them, rejecting role themselves, and maybe some are attempting to mitigate homosexual feelings. But I still think the big one is antirejection of one's own self or ego, as my patient put it. And if mama is involved, I think it's less of a sexual yen for her, than a powerful feeling of needing closeness. And if old hurts as very young children were strong enough, closeness may not even be enough. There may even be a feeling of need to be one with her—to climb right back inside and to be safe—safe from rejection by others and even more so, from rejection and hate poured on by one's own self.

A large glass aquarium of clear water—just that, nothing else, is quite beautiful. Add an air stone and or bubbles from a filter and the bubbles and ripples add to its beauty. Ten or twelve goldfish (to a fifty-five gallon tank) especially long finned fish, all and any colors—reds, golds, blacks, mottled, orange, etc., make it unbeatable and yet throughout the years, the temptation to add a stone or a little house or something persists. Yet I know how goldfish can destroy themselves wedging between things or scraping bodies or fins. I also know that most stones exude minerals, some of which can be dangerous.

Perhaps writing this book has in some way stimulated some creative ability in this area, because tonight it came to me. I have a number of very beautiful, old, glass paperweights that were given to me years ago, which I don't use. They are heavy and immovable, perfectly smooth, glass and therefore neutral and free of salts and chemicals—in short, perfect for the tank. But then I had a distinct sense of reluctance—more than that, inhibition! I explored it. What came to me was that they were unnatural—that they would never be found in a natural goldfish pond. But clay little houses and bridges are unnatural, too. But I had seen those in tanks, and I had never seen glass paperweights. I overcame my need to conform, my inhibition, and gave way to my creative urge.

The light shining through the paperweights—one red, the other orange—looks strange, unfamiliar and very beautiful. I came back to the tank several times this evening to look at the effects of the paperweights. Each time I headed in its direction, I had a small feeling of disquietude. It was the unfamiliarity of the paperweights in that strange place. My need to conform, how powerful this kind of thing is, was obviously still strong. But each look at the tank made the juxtaposition of the paperweights in a goldfish aquarium less unfamiliar and less strange. It is late at night now and as I write this and look at the tank, I feel that my disquietude is completely gone. I have a sense of fulfillment. I have finally found the something else to put in the tank and the newness and sense of creative originality feels very fulfilling, especially since I have no history whatsoever of any kind of visual artistry. I wonder how much the latter has to do with inhibition— and the difficulty with adaptation to anything new.

They are sexual creatures after all, though it may be difficult to differentiate males from females at times other than when they are in the mating season. (At that time, the male—only the male—has small white dots on his head and on the section of wings closest to his body.) Most fancy goldfish, orandas, lionheads, pearl skins, celestials, bubble eyes, black moors, and so on, usually look fat, and this applies to both males and females so their shape is no help in differentiating sexes. This fat look is due to the normal shape of the abdomen which bulges in all directions. Goldfish are egg layers, and will usually only mate if they are alone. They like their privacy. Mating consists of some chasing about, dropping eggs and the male dropping sperm on the eggs. There may be some body contact during these activities, but calling it lovemaking is stretching a point. In fact, goldfish don't seem to touch very much at all, except when they accidentally bump into each other and even then they appear rather oblivious to each other. Yet some fish seem to form some kind of attachment because they will spend an entire lifetime following each other about the tank and almost always will manage to be in each other's presence. Sometimes they will kiss each others' bodies, but this seems to be part of a random search for food rather than any sign of affection. I'm reminded of kissing gouramies—small, typical, home tropical fish who meet mouth to mouth repeatedly and actually kiss but I don't know what function this mouth to mouth contact has. Do goldfish feel? What do they feel? I don't know. I know so little about the feelings of other species. Knowing about how tiny their brains are, and how simple their nervous systems are compared to our own and that they are cold-blooded creatures doesn't really tell me much. Despite the latter information I sometimes feel that they feel more than we know. Is it possible that they feel panic when they are transferred from one tank to another? I have met people who swear that goldfish die of fright. If they have been in the dark for a long time, and the bright light is put on suddenly, they often dash about as if frightened. Is this pure reflex or is it a more complicated kind of fear approaching our own response to sudden change? Do they have much tactile sensation? Can they feel great pain? And how much of this is my own projection and a kind of anthropormorphizing?

On my part, and that of so many goldfish fanciers I've talked to, it is strange and maybe not so strange that we like goldfish, fishing and eating fish. What can be crueler to a fish from his point of view than hooking him, killing him and eating him? Yet we go to great pains to care for them and provide homes for them if they are the right ones. But don't we more or less do this with our own species, too? And the caring for them—it isn't really for them, it's for us—we care for them so that we can enjoy having and looking at them. As for catching them and eating them, when they are not gold, but some other kind of fish—perhaps all this is a kind of primitive love and more connected than compartmentalized and disconnected. Perhaps I'm being somewhat Freudian, but these are free associations and I'm not applying nor implying any moral equivocations whatsoever. So—is this desire to take in with line and hook, with mouth, with eyes in the case of goldfish, and with hands (they will come to the same spot to be fed and it can feel nice to pet their heads—though I don't know what they feel), a kind of primitive love—a childlike desire to absorb and add the loved object to self?

In any case, I look at them now, and at the bubbles and at the water and at the sandwich glass paperweights and all theorizing drops off and I feel that sense of inner free floating oneness with them and in this moment, this now, I feel good.

She made the connection between her repressed anger and her depression almost at once. She said that she understood that "I have to let my anger out rather than turn it in on myself." I think she has the gut feel of this and it's good, but it's also simplistic. What is she so angry about and what are her feelings about feelings and particularly about anger and what causes this inability to feel it and to express it and on and on it goes and there's a great deal to explore and to understand.

I have written about a storehouse of repressed angry feelings in the *Angry Book,* but this was for the sake of practical application. More and more I feel that feelings can't be stored at all. They can only be felt in the present. When we experience feelings of the past they are not really feelings which have been sitting there and are of the past at all. They are related to the past. We are feeling *now* about whatever current associations we may have to past events. As for repression—repression is like a side road for expressing feelings. What I mean is, that repressing is itself a way of discharging feelings. In terms of energy discharge, it doesn't matter whether we are dealing with implosion or explosion. The energy—in this case emotional energy—will be discharged either way, though implosion may be more painful. This is important because it means that analysis must not only consist of discharge of feelings related to past events. If it consists of only that, it is endless and will produce relatively little growth and change because the person in question will keep reacting the same way to newly accumulated events.

A real change can therefore only take place by understanding and changing ways of feeling and behaving and this can only be done by understanding how we view ourselves and all related people and events in our lives. This too of course must take place on a gut feeling level. When it does, real change is possible. The woman I saw in consultation will not only be able to feel and discharge her anger in a more self-constructive way. She will also perhaps change herself vis-à-vis herself and many situations in her life so that she becomes healthily more peaceful (not deadened or resigned), and less prone to anger generally.

We were at some friends' house last night. He is an extremely punctual and punctilious man. Before we left, he reminded us that the clocks must be moved ahead one hour at two A.M. tomorrow morning. I asked him what he thought the effect would be if newspapers, radio, television and so on, said to "move your clocks ahead *about* one hour *some time during the day tomorrow* instead of *one hour* at *two A.M. tomorrow.*" He just didn't understand. His wife understood at once and laughed. She said that at first there would probably be chaos. People would be frantic waiting for other people to arrive at appointments who would be very late or who already arrived and left. Transportation schedules would be entirely disrupted. Media and entertainment programs would be completely off schedule and would run into each other. She said it all sounded "delicious" to her, and she looked pointedly at her husband who by this time looked visibly anxious and annoyed. I told her that the normally precise Swiss are not very strict about television program time and if a program goes over time unexpectedly, they don't seem to care. She said that in that case her esteem of the Swiss goes up considerably. Her husband was really sweating now but said nothing. She said that the long-term results of being utterly casual about time would be wonderful. "The pressure would be off." "People would ease up in everything they do." "They'd stop being robots and would become humanized." At this point, I told her about my laughing at the clinic board meeting over the uniformity of the wristwatches. We all started laughing and for a full ten minutes couldn't stop—except her husband. When we finally stopped laughing we left and once again he very soberly reminded us to move our clocks ahead one hour at two A.M. tomorrow morning.

She said that she had relationships in which self-assertion played no role at all because with those people there was almost never an adversary position. She said she had other relationships in which she had to periodically assert herself. There were still others, some in business and some others in her social life, in which asserting herself was almost a constant necessity. I asked her why, and she said that it was because in these, though the relationships had value, she found herself in an adversary position. I said that I have had relationships like that and I found that some were not as worthwhile sustaining as I origi-

117

nally thought, and I felt no loss at breaking them off. In others, I continued to assert myself always and I discovered that maintaining this pride in *always asserting myself* was a considerable strain. I therefore tried to not assert myself at least in some of the issues involved. This was not easy at first as I had become used to hating myself whenever I "did not stand up for my position." At first I couldn't prevent the self-recriminations following "my surrenders." But after a while it got much easier. In fact, after a short time, I was able to just let go, capitulate at will without any subsequent self-berating attacks at all. I found that my judgment was excellent, that is, I didn't lose a thing in not asserting myself in the particular issues I chose to surrender. Once I put down my pride in *always*—and I think *always* is the key word here— asserting myself, I had a choice as to whether or not the issue called for assertion on a practical level, or surrender. Having this choice and exercising it gave me enormous relief and saved me a great deal of time and energy. I was no longer the slave of "the principle of the thing." I had discovered the strength of surrender—at least occasional surrender. She said she understood. I told her this was not going to be easy—that giving up chronic self-assertion was even harder than giving up chronic surrender and compliance, even though they both came from poor self-esteem. She said she understood this also.

REFLECTIONS IN A GOLDFISH TANK

I was at a gathering last night and a conversation took place about pornography. One woman there, old (eighty-eight), but also young and attractive, told us that she likes it, pornography, and always has—even relatively bad stuff—and if it's really good, she likes it all the more. Someone asked her what "really good" means, and she said stuff that is artistic, that conveys powerful feelings and puts others in touch with those feelings—sexual feelings.

I asked her what her opinion is as to why we are attracted to it. Is it just curiosity? Is it a way we measure ourselves? Is it an attempt to relieve our own sexual urges and needs through a kind of vicarious acting out? Is it a way to stimulate ourselves so as to bring feelings to life which are relatively deadened? Is it an attempt to heighten feelings—to make strong feelings still stronger? She said that she thought it was all these and still more. She told us that she often wondered why we weren't content to let what was dying in us just die or "let the dormant be dormant—but we are not." She said that in her case she wanted to feel the old feelings again—"the real old ones, when I was very young and felt exquisitely alive and didn't know it. Now I know I don't feel that way anymore, but I try and the quest is fun." She said that pornography—particularly "good stuff," which is not too mechanically concrete and allows her to use her own imagination at least in small measure—helps to maintain a good "synthetic feeling" even though it's not as good as the original "way back when." She seemed young and vi-

119

tal to us all. There was nothing synthetic about her that I could detect. The rest of us agreed that we felt older than her—not wiser, just older.

I heard the music from the show "Pal Joey" on the radio this morning, and I recalled sitting in the garden in Brooklyn listening about fifteen years ago to the same album and feeling nostalgic for the time I first heard the same music ten years before that. How Brooklyn has changed in those twenty-five years. It used to be so peaceful and green and of course how much younger we were. I thought about the young old lady of the other night and the business of feelings changing and recalling moods which are really, I suppose, symphonies of feelings. This nostalgia for nostalgia is surely evidence of much time passing and being, as the French say, of "a certain age." Seems to me that music, like no other art form, can bring back memories and especially memories of moods and feelings and various ambiances we've experienced in our lives. Music we hear for the first time can be enjoyed for its immediacy, though perhaps on an unconscious level it too hooks up to associations of old melodic associations and feelings and moods from the past related to whatever story it somehow conveys to us. But there's no question about old music and what it gives us each time we hear it—its immediacy stirring up current feelings and also bringing back old ones. I recall now, how as teenagers with very short pasts, we'd sit around recalling "old times," each of us saying, "Do you remember this one?" and enjoying the nostalgic feelings it brought even at that early age.

Theodore Isaac Rubin, M.D.

Eight of us, all old friends, went out to an excellent Chinese restaurant last night. The food was good and the discussion was even better. Everybody had a good deal to say and all of us were interested enough to listen, too. We had excellent Japanese rice beer and all of us felt particularly warm and good. The evening was a thoroughly enjoyable one in all ways, and when we left I had the feeling that we had had a great deal of each other. There had been plenty of communication, plenty of relatedness and good fellowship. We were satisfied and needed no more from each other. Therefore, the good-byes were appropriately short with no need to hang on in order to get more. But I think this kind of short "good-bye" without affection, nicety or embroidery is only possible with strong friendships—real ones in which satisfying exchanges take place.

REFLECTIONS IN A GOLDFISH TANK

We got into a discussion of what makes for good family mental health. Of course, how well the people relate, not stifling feelings, a fair degree of health on the part of the individuals involved—all this and much more was discussed.

But then when I left, I thought about it some more. All people are neurotic to some degree. Assume we take this as a base factor which no family escapes. Is there any other prime factor which determines whether or not a general family influence will be healthy or sick?

What occurred to me is that there may indeed be a big factor. That is the unconscious conglomerate decision on the part of each family as to whether they are going to live mainly influenced by each member's sickest aspects and characteristics or healthy ones. It's also a question of whether the family will avail itself of the talents of its members or ignore them. I'm sure this "decision" as I call it, isn't pure and I'm sure that this "decision" is based on the kind of communication and the relative influence of the various members relative to each other. But a ratio or balance is, I think, eventually arrived at in which the family will mostly, if not entirely, tap the assets or the liabilities of its members, and this is what I'm calling its "decision" for sickness or for health, even though influences of both are invariably present. The "decision" will determine the general mystique and influence of the family in the minds of its members. It will determine whether or not the family influences in the direction of emotional security, self-esteem, confidence and openness in relating to others or to self-hate, suspiciousness, inadequacy and paranoia.

I know one family in which the members live according to the father's (and husband's) stinginess and fear of people and the mother's (and wife's) hysteria and hypochondriasis. They have ample money, but lead a tight frugal existence and have relatively little to do with others on a social level. They also live in chronic fear of illness and are constantly being dragged to various doctors. *But* other possibilities are inherently there. The father is a capable and hard worker and has a certain solidity and confidence in his health and that of his children. The mother is an outgoing and gregarious person and is also quite capable of making good judgments in the realistic handling of money. How different the life of this family would be if each used his and her healthy influence to help the other and to help the family instead of catering to the sickest aspects of each other and themselves! In thinking about this family, I also think of so many others I know in which relatively healthy members are sacrificed for the sickest one. I know groups in which the sickest member sets the standards, values and frame of reference. I suppose this is what happens in any unduly sick organization. This includes whole societies in which terribly disturbed demagogues appeal to the sickest aspects of each member of the population who for that terrible moment abandons all the potentially mitigating healthy forces in himself.

REFLECTIONS IN A GOLDFISH TANK

Sam now has a hard time scrambling for food, swimming on the side the way he does. I once met a fish dealer who told me that he killed fish that he thought were too sick to recover. I didn't go into his store again. He told me he did it because he didn't want the fish to suffer. I don't believe that. I believe that he couldn't stand his own suffering and anything that in any way awoke it in him. I think the same is true of shooting horses. People can't tolerate less than a perfectly healthy, graceful running animal. He represents a certain aspect of our idealized image, and this must not be tampered with.

I remember listening to a paper a psychiatrist gave about a patient he had treated for some years. During the course of the treatment the patient at one point became very depressed and the therapist referred him to another psychiatrist, who gave him electroconvulsive treatments. I was appalled because I realized that this kind of treatment was not indicated. It was given because the doctor could not tolerate the pain in himself that the patient's distress evoked.

It isn't enough to be able to stand our own pain. We must be able to tolerate pain in others—in loved ones and in patients this may be much more difficult than our own suffering. I suppose it's particularly important in physicians, otherwise they may unconsciously make some bad decisions.

Sam's inability to right himself hurts me, but he is in no danger from my empathy.

Tonight I was thinking about liking people. I mean why do we like certain people? I feel this is a chemistry, which is impossible to analyze and which has very little justice in it. I have liked people and still do who are stingy, narcissistic, self-serving and even psychopathic. There are even those I like who are relatively dull and boring and others who have little or no sense of humor. There are also people I like who are altruistic, gentle, kind, intelligent, interesting, and so on. But there are also some with every seeming virtue, whom I don't particularly like at all. I'm sure there are people who feel the same way about me. What is it about? I don't know. Maybe it has much to do with aspects of ourselves which we are reminded of which we have and haven't made peace with. Or maybe it's simpler than that. Perhaps there's

126

some small aspect or characteristic—a certain bit of human stuff we are open to pick up somehow in certain people which makes us like them and we are somehow closed to in other people however well their virtues add up to a big score on a logical level. Or maybe it's none of these at all—maybe it's just a question of all kinds of reminders of other people we liked or disliked in the past. Or perhaps it's a question of trust, but it can't be that because there are a number of people I like who, in fact, I don't particularly trust, and some who I trust who I don't like. No—I really don't understand—no more than I understand why I like certain foods, paintings, music, books, smells, sounds, looks, and so on, and dislike others. I suspect the chemistry is complex and has to do with the deepest substance of ourselves. I'll say this though— my taste in most things remains fairly consistent, but with people, I've changed my mind from time to time. I seldom change from liking to disliking them, but I have changed from disliking to liking them and maybe this has to do with increased familiarity, exchange of feelings and trust. Maybe it's the rather narcissistic business of giving certain people something of ourselves—investing emotion in them and then caring about them because they now contain something of ourselves. But why do we make the investment in some and not in others? I can apply Freudian theory here as regards early history and associations to parents and siblings and so on but these explanations don't leave me satisfied. This is one of those issues where it feels better to not understand rather than to accept a theoretical stand which doesn't feel right. I'll just go on disliking and liking, and sometimes I'll change from disliking to liking and at those times I do feel particularly good—not virtuous—just a good feeling.

Today I heard from Jim's wife that he has to have his gall bladder out. *But* he's not going to have it done in the hospital in which he himself is the chief of ear, nose and throat. This despite the fact that the hospital in which he's on staff is an excellent, medical school-affiliated nonprofit hospital and one in which his colleagues, the resident staff and the nursing staff love him and would take superb care of him. He is instead going to a small, private and decidedly inferior hospital, despite his surgeon's advice. The surgeon is a colleague also on the staff at the university-affiliated hospital and explained the advantages of post-operative care at the larger place. Jim told his wife that he didn't want the staff to see him as a patient. He said it was as simple as that. He admitted that it had nothing at all to do with undermining his authority, and he knew very well that many of the doctors on staff had been hospitalized there at various times in their lives. He said it was a question of pride and this was the way it had to be. But does Jim know how sick his pride is—probably much sicker than his gall bladder? It would be interesting to explore his feelings about patients and about being sick and helpless. Does all this stir contempt in him for them and hatred for himself when he finds himself in their position? Does he feel that it is a disgrace for doctors to get sick? Are doctors, in his mind, supposed to sustain a state of omnipotent health?

Theodore Isaac Rubin, M.D.

I am reminded of a psychoanalyst friend of mine who told me how, when he was at a large professional meeting, he suddenly suffered severe chest pains. He was one of the discussants of a paper being given and was sitting on stage waiting for his turn at the microphone. The chest pains got worse, and he said he felt a sense of embarrassment rather than fear. He never got to the microphone because the pain got so severe that he finally leaned over and told a colleague sitting next to him about it, who was also waiting to speak. The other analyst stopped the meeting and at this point my friend said he thought his embarrassment "would kill" him. An ambulance was called for, and my friend was taken out on a stretcher. The pain was now excruciating and he had difficulty catching his breath, but he felt that he wanted the cover on the stretcher pulled over his head so that the crowd on the sidewalk wouldn't see him "that way" as he was "loaded on the ambulance." On arrival at the hospital, he was immediately examined and placed in the intensive care unit. He still felt embarrassed by it all and since has come to the conclusion that his embarrassment was based on pride invested in never being helpless, which covered up profound feelings of self-effacement— "all this fuss made over me." In the intensive care unit he was told to lie flat and to try not to move. But despite a heavy injection of morphine and an oxygen mask he sat up halfway and tried to joke with the nurse. He said he later realized that this was a further attempt to cover up his embarrassment and probably also to fool himself into believing that there was nothing really seriously wrong. He said he was certainly aware of the embarrassment, but only theorized about the denial of serious illness. The nurse on duty came over to him and said and he remembered her words, "Doctor, you are now a patient, lie back and be one, keep quiet, lie still and let us save your life." He said that he suddenly realized that this was a life and death issue and that here he was embarrassingly joking away his one and only life. The embarrassment and denial stopped at once. From that moment on he became a model patient. The nurse had crushed "my insane pride and saved my life." As it turned out he had in fact suffered a serious heart attack and went on to an excellent recovery. This man is now in relatively good health and he says it is because he continues to take proper care of himself. We agree that had his pride in omnipotence continued he never would have survived the initial attack. But even if he did, the lack of self-care which would have surely followed would have resulted in an early death.

My patient told me how "You can't fight city hall." This had to do with a complicated case involving a very high real estate tax, but I also knew that this man had a long-standing history of instant capitulation to authority. Then I thought of my own past history of compulsively fighting anything at all that even remotely seemed authoritarian. I didn't want to project my difficulties to him. Perhaps this was indeed one of those times which called for victory through surrender. But in my heart of hearts, I knew this was not a case of compulsive self-assertion and for the first time in many years I thought of my father and the United States Navy.

At the beginning of World War II, some twelve or fifteen of us, all students at Brooklyn College, and all Jewish, applied for the Naval officers training program. We filled out applications—went down to 90 Church Street (headquarters for the N.Y. Naval district) for intelligence tests and interviews and received rejections a few days later—all of us. We attributed the rejections to anti-Semitism and to the fact that we attended a free nonelite school famous for its liberalism and even radicalism. The school was also at the time well known for its extremely high academic standing. We may well have been right because any number of people we knew—mostly non-Jewish from other schools in the city—were readily accepted into the program. Of course we had no proof beyond that, and we didn't know if this was a local policy or a general one throughout the service.

Up to that point, as I said, I was fairly rebellious in regard to authoritarian pressure but the U.S. Navy was something else. This was different. I was in awe and I felt there was no way to stand up to the Navy. All my friends at Brooklyn College felt the same way. But my father took a different attitude entirely. He said that there was no U.S. Navy. At first I didn't understand him at all. He said that we unfortunately come to regard the Government, the Navy, the Nation, the City as larger than life, as larger than the people who comprise it and as Godlike and invincible. He said that the Navy consisted of ships and people and that both were vulnerable and movable. He said that he was going to have a talk with the commandant of the Naval district over at 90 Church Street. I thought of the men who interviewed me, the uniforms, the gold braid, the formality, the austere offices, the huge building itself and then I thought of my father, his Russian Jewish accent (my own self-hate) and I tried to persuade him otherwise. I told him this was not like discussions in back of his drugstore—this was the United States Navy after all. He replied that the discussions in back of the store were surely more difficult and of higher intellectual caliber.

My father got the appointment with the commandant and one day later I received a letter to come down to be reevaluated. I did and I was "retested" and sent to the commanding officer who congratulated me on being admitted to the program. He said that my initial rejection was a mistake of some kind and that I was exactly the kind of young man the Navy wanted in its program—"six feet three, strong, healthy, athletic, and that I had scored perfectly on the IQ test." The latter was easy as this was the second time I took it. I went into the Navy and did in fact become a deck officer. Most of my friends who were initially rejected reapplied, and were also accepted and eventually successfully commissioned.

What did my father tell the commanding officer? He said that his son was completely eligible, six feet three, on the wrestling team and a champion handball player, very intelligent, and that he (my father) viewed his rejection very badly and suggested an immediate review of the case. He said that if this wasn't done he'd know where to go. He told me that the commanding officer couldn't be more polite, placated him and told him that there had probably been some mistake. I asked my father where he would have gone if his request was turned down. He said that he would have found some way and some one to protest to effectively, but that this wasn't important. Authoritarians and especially prejudiced authoritarians always feel shaky about their own positions. To tell them that you know where to go is the thing—to leave it vague and to let their imaginations do the rest. I marvelled at him and realized that he was right. There was no Navy after all—just people, and with people recourse is almost always possible.

REFLECTIONS IN A GOLDFISH TANK

If we could only learn to think less and to feel and do more. If we could only go through periods of no thinking at all—a kind of sustained meditation—seeing, hearing, smelling, feeling and doing. So much of the thinking is nothing more than useless anticipation; debilitating and useless worrying; boring and fatiguing ruminating. So little "doing" requires planning or any kind of verbal thinking at all. It only requires active participation and involvement. Most of the things we need or want to do require only the doing itself and no thought at all, most of which is used as a delaying mechanism and as a self-sabotaging process which wastes both time and energy. I remember signs on desks, blackboards and walls which said *Think,* and I think we need signs which say *Anti-Think* and *Do.* But of course all this excessive thinking we do serves a purpose. The purpose is to keep us from our true feelings and the true feel of ourselves. The purpose is to obfuscate and to rationalize and to promote illusions about ourselves and the world. The more honest we get with ourselves—really honest with all of ourselves including all which is less than ideal, the more we can do away with useless mind-busywork, and the more we can do—directly do in the real service of our real selves. Perhaps one way to do it is to refuse to look back or ahead but to be involved in only the here and now of it. *Now* is usually the time that permits the least thought and promotes the most involvement with actual doing. But the struggle for real self and against perfection must ultimately take place and has to go on as a continuing proess if we really want to grab hold of *now*—the only time there really is. And even in this regard, we must realize that success is only of the human variety which means that it's relative. But to whatever extent we succeed, there's a kind of inner peace and rest that prevails as well as a return to oneness and spontaneity which makes formal meditation exercises and other such modalities unnecessary.

This morning I thought the new oranda I bought had ich (which is very contagious), and so I started to imagine I saw it on some of the other fish already, too. Fortunately, I was wrong, but there's no question that each introduction of a new fish brings its risks both to the rest of the fish and to him, too. But of course it also brings new color, new movement and new excitement and interest. I suppose it's no different than the introduction of a new person to any group or a new idea to a status quo of established ideas. But I felt down-hearted about it, and anything but philosophical. Changing a tank full of water is no fun. In that moment I felt that I knew nothing about these fish after all. I was sick of taking care of them and ready to chuck the whole thing. But the moment passed, and it would have passed anyway, even if the fish were sick. Of course as with humans, it's important not to crowd them, to give them room. Young fish are inexpensive, but my own experience has been that only a small fraction of them make it to adulthood even under ideal conditions. I suspect that every large older fish the breeder sells represents one of a batch most of which never make it to adulthood.

I suppose fancy goldfish are stuck, and we who have bred them into existence are responsible for them. With their long fins and round low-slung bodies, they wouldn't last minutes in a free pond or lake. I suppose man has bred a whole world full of dependent creatures like this—dogs, horses, cats, though I periodically hear of animals readapting to a wild state. Of course I immediately think of that fancy apartment house and it occurs to me that some of us have gotten pretty fancy and vulnerable, too. It is not difficult to forget the difference between needs and wants so that needs become escalated way beyond what they really are. And it gets very difficult even to think of giving up anything we once had and come to think of too easily as absolute necessity. It takes no time at all to become addicted to all kinds of status and pride positions so that coming down to earth is viewed with horror and occurs with a terrible crash. Unlike the oranda, this kind of blowing oneself up to a state of confused and empty pretension only makes us frightened and vulnerable and doesn't add to attraction or beauty at all.

This morning I woke up thinking that perhaps I would sort out all the old photographs I've taken over the years. But I felt that I really didn't want to do this. I preferred to go out for a walk. As a matter of fact I've been meaning to do this photo-sorting for years and have never done it. I then realized I never did want to do it. I thought about doing and thinking again. The fact is that I've done the things I wanted to do, and what I haven't done were things I never really wanted to do in the first place. I decided not to sort out the photos—not now and probably not ever. I decided to rid myself and free myself from any to-do items listed in my mind that have been there for more than a very short time.

About my friend who had the coronary occlusion, the massive heart attack. He told me of the excellent care he got once he allowed himself to receive it—without embarrassment. He was sedated most of the time, and between the morphine and sedatives, he said that he was completely anxiety-free. Of course everything was done for him on a physical level too, so that there was no possibility at all of any strain. It saved his life. But was it this direct? He told me that the combination of the realization of how dangerous his position was, plus the extraordinary care, permitted him to let go—to surrender all of his inner dictums, all of his shoulds and should nots, re-criminations, worries and anticipations. In short, he was able to neutralize his super ego—his conscience. He told me it was as if he told that part of himself, "Look you better lay off now—otherwise I will die and you will get nothing at all out of me—nothing. Also, other people are in charge now, so we have to surrender to them, to let go completely." Yes, in other terms we could say that he invalidated any quest for glory, any quest for self-idealization. He had, for the time of his hospitalization, learned to accept himself without quests for perfection of any kind, without frills and even without goals. He was satisfied to just live. He learned the lesson well, and said he is still doing it up to a point, but admits that some of the inner tyrannical drives are back in power, and that he certainly doesn't feel as anxiety-free as he did in the hospital. In any case, it is now several years since the attack—and he is alive and fairly well. But what was the attack an attack on? Perhaps it can be seen as more than a heart attack, but also an attack on self (the heart attack) and then a counterattack on sick pride and neurotic striving. The counterattack succeeded! Death was prevented. But could the initial attack have been prevented? Supposing he received, or any of us receive ICU (intensive care unit), care and treatment with full hospitalization before heart attacks occur? Could we let go then or would we still need badly damaged hearts to bring us to our senses? Because that's the way it seems to be. We seem to allow ourselves real peace only when we are so sick that no other option is possible. Again and again I have seen people in states of bad anxiety and deep depression who hope for severe physical illness which would serve as an ally to help stop their terrible self-flagellation—a self-damaging martyrdom kind of black-mail to use against devastating self-hate. What a strange ally and how terrible that heart attacks and worse are necessary before we can give ourselves some right to live in peace with ourselves. My friend and I discussed all this. We certainly have the scientific laboratory means and also interview techniques to measure stress. Could we prevent heart attacks and strokes by instituting exactly the same intensive and then prolonged care which would have been given had the attack actually taken place? He said the physical care might help somewhat—the sedation would prevent anxiety for a while. But without the attack and the terrible danger it brings, even the drama of the attendant treatment situation, would not be enough to put down all the shoulds and worries and compulsive ambitions, and so on. He told me that he doubted that we could get more than very few people into the hospital at all without an actual devastating physical onslaught. He smiled and admitted that there are times now when he knows that his own stressful situation has become dangerous. He uses the heart attack he has had to force himself to go on vacations more often than he has before the attack. But even in this, he doesn't always succeed. "There are so many *important* things to be done," and he honestly knows he would only go into a hospital to be treated for an attack, but not to prevent one. He knows there is nothing really more important that he does in terms of himself, his family and his patients, too, than to go on living, but he admitted sadly that the "letting go," the getting off the "driven road" (being driven) was very difficult to do without the threat of death as an ally. He also theorized that most of us have a kind of childish omnipotence in operation, too—a foolish belief that it can't really happen to us and this is an enemy against which very big ammunition is needed. He said that he gave up smoking at the time of the attack and that he never went back to it, so this at least indicates a constructive inroad of consequence.

Reflections in a Goldfish Tank

Our hosts took us out to a very lavish restaurant last night. We were twelve couples. The evening was divided into two periods. The first two-thirds of the evening was spent eating dinner in a large dining room at three different tables. People were seated only with people they had not met before—once again couples were split up. For the last third of the evening, we moved into a much larger ballroom-sized kind of living room, for champagne, coffee, desert and music. In this room, couples were reunited and sat wherever they liked. People who had not met during the first part of the evening were now introduced to each other, so by the end of the party everyone had met everyone else.

I had dinner seated next to an actress who was known to have had fair success in films, plays and television. She had never become a well-known star, and I had not seen her before. She was extremely attractive, dressed in a relatively revealing, obviously expensive and tasteful red gown and she wore a great deal of jewelry. She was about forty years old, red-haired, with very pale skin and light eyes and spoke in a highly cultivated British accent. She was clearly the star of our table. Her voice, her accent, her gestures were all somewhat stagy and dramatic. Everything about her was a bit overdone. But there was nothing unpleasant about her. In fact, she looked quite beautiful and all of us at the table, men and women alike, enjoyed looking and listening to her as we ate for the first hour. There was almost no other conversation, and she wasn't engaged in any kind of actual dialogue either. It

143

was more of a performance and audience-participation kind of hour. I marveled at her ability because, while she got all of our attention and we were all quite happy to look and to listen to her, she told us nothing at all of herself. She was very sexy-looking and did have a lively husky voice and interesting accent.

After about an hour, or a bit more, had passed, she asked what kind of work I did. I told her that I was a psychiatrist. She hardly seemed to hear me. Several minutes later, our host came to our table, he had been seated at the other one, to see how we were doing. Before he left he told the actress that I had written *Lisa and David*. A profound change took place immediately! She left center stage at once. She took my hand and kissed me on the cheek. As if on signal she somehow abruptly released the other couples because they now separated into pairs and were all having their own conversations. Her British accent was gone and with it went the husky voice. The gestures were gone too as well as the contrived manner. She spoke in a very low, pleasant voice. Her accent was decidedly American (New York and traces of midwest), and her face, more beautiful now, took on a soft glow and a serious expression. Her eyes filled with tears and she told me that *David and Lisa,* which the film had been called, moved her more than any film she had ever seen. She had read the book several times and had loved it. She wanted to know all about me and my work and family and listened attentively as I answered her many questions. She told me much about herself, her childhood, an arduous career and much struggling and both happiness and pain through the years. She couldn't be more real, more serious, articulate and intelligent—an altogether attractive and quite beautiful person. The metamorphosis was complete. She never did go back to center stage in that room and we all completed our dinner as couples, in small isolated conversations rather than in overall large ones.

Later on our host led us to the larger room where everyone who hadn't met before was introduced to everyone else. This time we sat wherever we liked—at small tables and small lounging couches and chairs. The woman I had talked to for several hours was gone. The actress was back. She was center stage again—the lovely British accent, the gestures, the contrived quality had all returned. When her eyes happened to glance in my direction, there was no evidence at all of recognition of our earlier conversation.

When the evening came to close, as we were leaving, she said to my wife and me that "we must see each other again." Going out the building, I couldn't make up my mind as to whether she said these last few perfunctory words as the real woman or the actress.

She asked me if writing is cyclic like everything else, and I said that it was.

I feel anxious and very uneasy and then something I want to write breaks into awareness. I start to write and the anxiety turns into exhilaration and before too long, into a state of relative comfort and equilibrium. Around the middle of the work, the process often gets arduous and this is the time which requires the most discipline—

sometimes a set routine to get it done. Toward the end, tension mounts, but this time it's a kind of pleasurable excitement, rather than anxious discomfort. Then when it's over, there's a short period of exhilaration, followed by a slightly longer period of relief and peace. This is followed by a sense of loss and mild depression, which in turn is followed by mounting tension and anxiety until the next work breaks through and completes the cycle.

She agreed that this pretty much described all aspects of life, and in her own experience the birth of each of her three children felt particularly like this cycle. We talked awhile about relationships, work, relaxation, sickness and health and both of us had some feeling for the cyclic flow involved. We both also wondered whether there was any way to break out of the cycle—particularly what we felt as creative cycles—to enhance free will and to be less controlled by forces of the unconscious. We decided that this would be very difficult. We spoke about the many creative ideas people had in dreams which led them to profound discoveries. I told her that I thought that control itself was antithetical to creative possibility and that discipline imposed too early could destroy a creative work before it gained sufficient momentum to come fully to life. I said that if we wanted to somehow break the autonomy of the cycle, it would probably take less will power and more openness. She said that most analysts she met went about in "well-analyzed little houses, but couldn't break out of their own houses." She said that there is not enough openness in people and we spoke of increasing openness to ourselves and all of our thoughts and feelings by struggling to suspend judgment values and moral equivocation based on a constricting self-idealizing cultural value system. I said that I thought one way to break into a lull period of the cycle and to start creative activity was to free-associate—just to let ideas and feelings and moods and thoughts come and to keep others coming each relative to those that preceded until patterns make themselves known. We agreed that this is not easy and as in psychoanalysis it again involves the smooth flow of acceptance of all aspects of self without the stopgap interruption of its "good" or its "bad" moral kinds of judgment.

REFLECTIONS IN A GOLDFISH TANK

Ellie and I were alone in the beach house about a week ago and she suddenly got very sick. It was either a virus or food poisoning. She's all right now, but she still feels a little weak.

She threw up all night and for several hours toward morning she retched almost continuously and brought up nothing at all because her stomach was quite empty by that time. She was extremely weak and dehydrated for the next two days and I gave her ginger ale and Coca-Cola, which was about all she could tolerate. It may have been a virus rather than food poisoning, because she had a high temperature and was achy, very sleepy and generally seemed quite toxic. I didn't give her aspirin that night because it would be too irritating to her stomach and so I sponged her with diluted vodka (we had no alcohol and the drugstore had closed hours earlier), to keep her temperature down. Toward morning it dropped from 103° to 100° and it didn't go back up the next night. She was extremely nauseated after the retching had passed and the Coca-Cola and ginger ale only helped a little. I found some Compazene pills in the closet but these started her retching again. Fortunately, there was no sign of an acute abdomen of any kind. Her belly was soft, but quite sore from all the heaving. She finally retained the Compazene, and the nausea disappeared. When the acute phase of this thing was over by the afternoon of the day after that night, she fell asleep and slept until the next afternoon—almost twenty-four hours.

While she slept, I thought. This was the first time I had

taken direct, physical, care of Ellie in the over thirty years we've been together. Actually, this was the first time I was this directly involved with the prolonged physical care of anyone at all. When our children had been ill, she took care of them and of me too, whenever I've been sick. Ellie has almost never been sick.

I felt good taking care of her, more than good, very good. While I was busy taking care of her I didn't think about it at all. I was too busy. I was completely involved, and yet with no thought at all I felt a great deal. I felt full of warmth and very soft, gentle and caring feelings for her and for myself too. About a day later, I woke up and had a strong urge to see my mother. I had a stronger feeling than I had in years, for the times she used to buy me different colored clay to mold when I was sick. Then I remembered for the first time in thirty or more years how she rubbed potatoes down to a mash to make pancakes for me and friends I brought home from school for lunch when I was in perhaps the second or third grade. I also recalled her promising once to make all the potato pancakes I could eat when I got better when I was very sick for a long time. She kept her promise, and I must have eaten a hundred of them and nearly got sick all over again. Ellie and I visited her yesterday and it was so different from so many of the other visits. I didn't feel restless or irritated with her complaints. I felt at peace, glad to be with her and much warmth for her, very similar to what I felt taking care of Ellie. Now as I write this it's not quite the same and yet some of it is still here with me. "It"—what is "it"? I think some mothering feelings have been generated in me. I could say fatherly, but it doesn't feel right. No, I think it's motherly all right, and perhaps I had to wait until now not to be threatened and to allow them to come to life in myself. Yes, I think I've got an inkling of what mothering feels like and I now know deep inside that it feels good.

My friend, a movie maker, asked me why I thought Sigmund Freud was able to do as much as he did in his life. He understood Freud's genius and his energy. I immediately thought of my own lack of energy and how Ellie takes so many loads off my shoulders which makes it possible for me to do much of what I want to do. But what my friend was really getting at was Freud's ability to stand up against all professional opinion contrary to his own at that time—more than that—to believe in himself—"to believe in his own greatness." I told him that I had read that Freud himself said that a man could be great if his mother believed in his potential for greatness. I told him that Freud's mother called her son "mine goldene Ziggy"—my golden Ziggy. My friend said very wistfully that he could well understand the impact and effect of a mother's early and sustained belief in a son's worth. He said he never had this. "No one ever called me 'goldene' anything," he said. He asked about me and I told him that I remembered my mother calling me by affectionate terms—"Little boy" and "little son" also "little father," but nothing golden and nothing related to belief in future greatness. I told him of my recent experience with Ellie and my memory of potato pancakes after being sick. He said that perhaps this was more important than the "goldene stuff." "Maybe it paved the way to be more human with one's self—less perfect and more human." But I thought and told him of my own painful struggles with pride and arrogance and self-idealizations in the past. He said that it might have been much worse without the pancakes. He then told me about his father—a very reserved, detached man. He said he couldn't understand why a man like that wants to have a family at all. I told him what my analyst, Nat Freeman, once told me—that "detached people" need people to be detached from. He said that when his father spoke at all, it was to tell him to conform with all existing conventions and standards, so as to not make waves, to be liked by all, so as to get along all right in this world "to be safe."

He asked and I told him that I did not have a single

memory of my father even suggesting that I conform to anything or anybody at all. He never told me to be like anyone else or asked the question so many of my patients remember, "Why can't you be like so and so?" My friend said that I was blessed inasmuch as I was asked to only be what I was rather than someone else. I told him that while this was true, and it was also true that I was never made to go to sleep at any given time and was free to go and come as I wished, my father and I had a great many fights. He asked about what and I told him about almost everything. We had so many differences of opinion and in many ways were much alike and I suppose highly competitive with each other. I told him about the importance of my mother's presence in those fights. Also, how I never quite got the feeling of full approval from him in anything I did. The implication my father managed to convey was that whatever it might be it was never quite good enough. My friend said he still envied me—he envied the fights, too—the friction and the freedom and the practice involved in speaking up and the experience of exchange "to exchange anything at all." I asked him about the lack of feeling that anything was ever good enough, and he said, "Yes, but even in that regard you were asked to do better in terms of yourself, not someone else and at least he cared." I told him that my father did care, and what he said was true, but that much of my early, sick, self-idealizing striving and self-hate too was a reaction to early lack of approval and my father's need for vicarious living through me, because I didn't remember his pushing himself very hard for personal triumph.

While I said this I marveled at how much in us from so long ago is settled and not settled at all—so much unfinished business which remains and which never is resolved. Then I told him that I do in fact value it all but that now—right now in looking back—the potato pancakes seem more valuable than anything else. Just before we parted he said once again—"No one ever even once called me 'mine goldene' anything."

The thought I had was—what if people didn't shake hands when they came into each other's presence and as they began to talk. What if instead, they held hands as they began to talk. Shaking hands—a quick shake and then a break in physical contact seems to be symbolic of fragmented conversation and lack of sustained, meaningful communication generally. Would it help if two people reached across—grasped each others' hands and held on to signal that they wanted to sustain prolonged contact for the purpose of real communication? Would it help or would it be so threatening that no feeling at all would be exchanged—only choppy remarks to cover frozen panic?

I thought about Freud and other "great men" and once again because I've thought about this many times, are there "great people" or just people some of whom have great talent or energy or both? There is a difference. One makes for competition and Godlike striving. The other makes for what Karen Horney called self-realization. One feeds narcissistic pride and self-glorifying idealization. The other feeds real self. One is never satisfied and is an endless climb (much like Sisyphus). The other is soul-satisfying.

Then I thought of all the people, particularly presidents and also organizations and cities and countries, too, and how we elevate them in our minds to Godlike status and then how hurt and bitter we feel when we find out that they were only people or groups of people, after all, and always did have human foibles. And the presidents and "great men" themselves—how often they are seduced by the public and by themselves into believing they are godlike—and the awful crashes down they inevitably suffer later on. Yes, we know that the gods have clay feet and yet we still insist on creating gods.

155

My movie-making friend is waiting for a decision on a project of his, and he asked me how come some people have so much difficulty making decisions.

I told him that for many people, this would represent a step forward. Many people are so compulsively driven by anxiety that they are not even aware that choices and options exist, let alone the possibility of free decision.

He asked about people who had several options, were fully conscious of their choices and still couldn't make up their minds and delayed endlessly.

I told him that I've come to realize that when I couldn't make a decision it really wasn't that I couldn't, but rather that I wouldn't. It was a kind of temper tantrum, because I couldn't satisfy all options. It was a refusal to give up anything and since the benefits of the options not chosen would be lost, I preferred a state of indecision. Also, indecision permitted me to sustain the illusion that there was a way to have it all after all. Of course refusal to surrender any of it usually results in losing all of it when the decision is out of our hands and made for us by someone else or change in outside circumstances. Surrender of all other options is usually as important as preference for one of them if an active decision is to be made at all.

We then went on to talk about films and actors and making movies generally. I told him that it was interesting how quickly we accept actors in different roles, and empathize and identify with each role an actor is in quickly and willingly, forgetting his last role, let alone the actual person he is. He thought that this is due to our roles. He thought that most of us are terribly afraid to step out of role and are more than willing to have actors do it for us.

We then spoke about people changing. I told him about people who tell me that they would like to get rid of their symptoms—anxiety, compulsions, phobias, depression—but that they don't want to change. I said this was impossible. Change is necessary for symptoms to be alleviated on any kind of sustained level. But aside from symptoms, I feel there is no choice in this matter of change anyway. We have to change. Complete stultification and holding to a status quo is not possible. Being alive is defined by the process of continuous change. Of course change can be in the direction of greater spontaneity or toward deeper inhibition and paralysis, but even the latter is change. I then told him of my son Jeff's question some years ago—"If people keep changing, then what stays the same to identify them as the same people?" I also told him that I've thought of trial and punishment for crimes committed in the past and if life is a process and change keeps taking place, then don't we in effect try and punish a man for a crime committed by a man who no longer exists?

We finally decided that the various ways of changing— the processes involved—identify people however much they change and grow and if these processes change enough, they the people may indeed be unrecognizable.

We also agreed that justice is a necessary expedient, but leaves much to be desired both in philosophical and psychological terms. We hoped that some day judgment

157

and punishment would give way to clinical study, treatment and prevention. But by this time we were both feeling rather high-handed, pretentious and stuffy and so we parted for the evening.

Speaking of change, the owner of a new fish store I discovered tried to sell me a very rare pair of goldfish I had never seen before. I didn't like them and I didn't buy them. I've changed. I wouldn't have bought them in the past either. But I would have been tempted. This time I wasn't tempted at all. Their looks did not appeal to me and that was the end of it. Their rarity was meaningless to me. The old pride that this would have once fed—to own a fish no one else has, etc., was gone—completely gone.

Reflections in a Goldfish Tank

She told us that she met a woman in the elevator yesterday she had been told about once whose name is Trudy.
They never met before, but in the short ride down in the
elevator they started to talk and it turned out that our
friend had heard of Trudy. She also knew that Trudy had
lost her husband six years ago. In the lobby just before
they parted, Trudy told her that her name "isn't really
Trudy at all. It's Gertrude. And it isn't even Gertrude. It's
Gittel. Only one person remembers me as Gittel—an old
woman, eighty years old, who used to be our neighbor
when I was a very little girl. I visit her every few months
and she calls me Gittel. I do this so that I won't forget
who I am." Our friend said, "So long Trudy." She
couldn't say "Gittel" or even "Gertrude" and doesn't

know why. Ellie said that perhaps it would seem contrived or patronizing and perhaps it was something she felt belonged only to the little girl Trudy once was and the old lady, no one else.

He told me that he behaved like a "perfect idiot" and I believe him. I told him that every genius has his idiot and occasionally the idiot, perhaps the most human part of himself, emerges and hopefully reminds him of his idiocy. I also told him that I believe that every idiot has a little germ of genius locked up in his idiocy. Sometimes that germ of genius blossoms a bit and desperately wants to come out but can't. The idiot won't let him and everyone else recognizing the idiot for an idiot won't let him let the flowering germ of genius come out. The result is a raging war in the idiot who becomes terribly agitated because no one will listen to what is happening to him.

But I should not have believed him! He didn't act like an idiot at all! He was much older than the nurse who took care of him after the operation. At one point he impulsively patted her on the cheek as she changed the dressing. He regretted it at once feeling "like an idiot," because it brought on so many confused feelings. He felt sexual; he felt very young; he felt fatherly and he felt very old and "a lot more that I just can't describe." Perhaps it was idiocy after all—the germ of genius in idiocy—in this case the blossoming out of so much that is all so human.

She said that the clue to her husband's character is that he raises vegetables instead of flowers, even though he loves flowers. "He just can't get himself to do anything that doesn't in some way have a utilitarian rationale." What really bothered her though, was his using her as his projected conscience. He has had several affairs over the years, and he told her about them in order to get absolution and relief. She doesn't care that much about it, except that if he uses her as his superego and his own superego is a powerful one, she knows that in part he will hate her, which will continue to drive him to other women for solace.

I agreed with her that he could use some help, and she and I did not schedule another appointment.

We just got home and it is very late. Ellie drove the car to our hosts' house and we both listened to the radio. An astronomer on the program told us that the stars were racing away from each other at an incredible speed. He said that there were huge empty spaces between islands of galaxies and that billions of years from now these galaxies and their stars would hardly be related at all, because of the trillions of miles between them. In that moment, driving in the dark, I understood the meaning of existential anxiety. I've read and discussed it many times in the past, but I never understood it until that moment in the car several hours ago. I felt it deep down in the core of my soul. It was different from the fear of death—even more pervasive and somehow more inclusive perhaps because I felt it not only for myself but in terms of our entire species. I felt my finiteness in juxtaposition to infinity and I never felt so small or vulnerable before in my life. The feeling passed very quickly and I was once again restored to the six-foot-three, two-hundred-and-ten-pound man sitting next to his wife listening to the radio in their big car. But following that moment, I also realized with more of my substance than ever before why pride is such a universal phenomenon. It must at least in part be a reaction to feeling so transient relative to those billions of years and billions beyond them. Pride is the tempest in the tea cup we create—pride and its diverse children—hierarchies of self-importance, power, prestige, etc., in an attempt to hide from the truth—to transcend finiteness. But it doesn't work. There is no transcending. Sustained comfort can only come of accepting being part of the whole, however small and fleeting our part may be, and this is not to say that for us our part is not very important. Of course it is, but it is only a small part of the universe and humility is the all-important antidote because without it we are rather foolish and self-hating in our synthetic self-importance and illusion of godlike omnipotence. Yes, the anti-pride position means survival. It's the only position in which we can be comfortable with ourselves and the enormity of it which we are only part of. If we insist on arrogating to ourselves all kinds of special positions that we don't have, we will surely be blotted out. The universe will help us do it to ourselves with nature's available atoms, poison air, etc. Yet, of course, pride persists, and we continue to promote it in the name of personal, local, family and national glory and greatness as we annihilate each other and ourselves. When we got to our friend's house, lights were shining brightly and everyone was dressed in their best and all was shining and gay. For a while I said nothing. How could I tell them of the infinite stretch of space I had just been part of? But after a while, most of the feeling passed, but I couldn't quite become part of the very nice evening.

REFLECTIONS IN A GOLDFISH TANK

On the way home I turned the radio back on but of course the program was over hours earlier. I can't imagine why I should have expected otherwise, since I heard it end myself.

This time there was music. Then there was a very beautiful song about kissing. As I've said earlier, some songs can bring back feelings of the past. Others can put us more in touch with *now*. Once in a great while a song comes along that can bring it all together and put us in touch with the *entire now of our lives*. Maybe it was my earlier feeling or the song or both but this song did it for me. It reminded me of a sweet kiss of twenty-eight years ago. Ellie had to wake me to keep an important appointment. It was in the afternoon. The sun was streaming in. It was mid-winter, Lausanne, Switzerland. She kissed me and it was the softest, warmest, gentlest kiss I've ever known. There have been many others before and since, but this kiss somehow has come to represent them all and this song brought back the gentle, mending feeling of that kiss. Ellie is fast asleep.

I'm tired now—this has somehow been quite an evening.

Why have we moved so many times? I hear that writers move a great deal—to recapture or to establish moods. I'm not consciously aware of this as a motivation. Perhaps in part it's due to the habit of moving, established when I was a child. I went to eight elementary schools, two high schools and eventually to five colleges. Have I been looking for Shangri-la? Whenever we've traveled to a new place I anticipated the possibility of some wonderful find, to which we will someday go back, to stay. Ellie always points out that I've been disappointed all the times in the past, and why not just enjoy what each place has to offer?—much less than my anticipations to be sure. More and more I'm able to do that. But we have moved so much. Why? No, it's not Shangri-la or heaven on earth I've been looking for. I think I now know what it's always been. It's been the feelings I had as a child. It's the multi-colored clay, the potato pancakes, the little clay house in the goldfish bowl. But goldfish hurt themselves scraping against clay houses. Was it ever there—the feelings about the clay house, or do I only now think that it was there then? I think it was partially there and in part it was there out of childhood imagination. A small part of the feeling lingers on, but I'm no longer that child, and I no longer have his imagination, and I can't bring what's left of that feeling into full bloom. No, there's no clay house in my tank but we have decided to keep the beach house after all. We are going to use it. We remember feeling somewhat down now and then and going there and

166

always feeling a little better. I remember feeling chaotic and stormy and standing out on the docks for an hour or so and calming down and feeling good.

The tank looks clear and quite beautiful. Sam seems to be getting to his food with greater ease.